12 SIMPLE SECRETS

ᵀᴼ STAYING CALM

in a crazy world

12 SIMPLE SECRETS

ᵀᴼ STAYING CALM

in a crazy world

GLENN VAN EKEREN

Orlando, Florida

12 Simple Secrets to Staying Calm in a Crazy World by
Glenn Van Ekeren

Published by HigherLife Development Services, Inc.
242 Westminster Terrace
Oviedo, Florida 32765
(407) 563-4806
www.ahigherlife.com

Cover Design: DaNita Naimoli

ISBN 13: 978-0-9793227-7-8
ISBN 10: 0-9793227-7-4

Scripture quotations marked NIV are from the Holy Bible, New
International Version. Copyright © 1973, 1978, 1984, International
Bible Society. Used by permission

09 10 11 12 13 — 8 7 6 5 4 3 2 1

Printed in the United States of America

Acknowledgments

THIS BOOK IS DEDICATED TO my father, Delmar Van Ekeren, and my father-in-law, Jon McClure, who fought courageous battles with cancer. They loved life with passion and—although cancer took their lives—their legacy lives on in spirit and memory.

INTRODUCTION

W̶E LIVE IN A STRESSFUL world. Today won't be a repeat of yesterday. The future is unknown. The pace of life is rapidly increasing. People are caught in the middle of a whirlwind of change. Many wait for the "good old days" to return, but it has no intention of making a comeback.

Wouldn't it be great if we could eliminate stress and pressure, saying good-bye to the problems of life? Guess what? It wouldn't be as great as we think. We would achieve very little, there would be no challenges to help us grow, and life would get boring. Stress, adversity, obstacles, and change are natural bits of life. The best way to survive and thrive today is to create the life we want despite the circumstances that surround us.

Each section in this book is designed to help you take charge of your life. The real-life stories, powerful quotes, doses of humor, and inspirational applications will encourage you to excel in every area of your life. You'll discover timeless wisdom to provide you with insights for achieving greater levels of success in your life. You will feel empowered to make a difference in how your day and life work out.

Feeling burned out, used up, overloaded, or just plain worn out isn't necessary. You can make the best of today's changing world, learn to capitalize on the opportunities change produces, and create a brighter future. Learn to anticipate, accept, adapt—even embrace—the challenges of change. Discover the skills and attitudes necessary to deal with the daily ups and downs. Take charge of your actions and reactions when situations hinder your ability to enjoy life in the fast lane.

I hope you'll be encouraged, motivated, and challenged as you read each selection. Dwell on one a day or devour the entire book in one sitting. Either way, you are bound to gain unshakable confidence and determination to make your life better today than it was yesterday.

Section One

EMBRACE CHANGE

Chapter 1

ENJOY LIFE IN TIMES OF CHANGE

> Just because we cannot see clearly the end of the road, that is
> no reason for not setting out on the essential journey. On the
> contrary, great change dominates the world, and unless we
> move with change we will become its victims.
>
> —John F. Kennedy[1]

CHANGE IS IRRITATING. I DISLIKE it. I resist it, wishing it
would go away.

As I write, our community leaders have decided to fix a
road between my home and my office. There are other streets I can
take, but I'm comfortable with my customary route. I continue to
take the streets that run into the detour, and I'm consistently upset
when I reach the impassable road.

I know, this minute irritation is nothing compared to the personal
and professional changes you are experiencing. Yet, isn't it often
the little things that get us? Expectations are unmet. Status quo is
shattered. Our comfort zone is suddenly pulled out from under us.
Nothing seems simple anymore, and we begin to blow things out of
proportion.

It doesn't take a psychiatrist to tell us that we all desire a sense of normalcy in our lives. How often have you heard a co-worker, spouse, or friend say, "I can't wait for things to get back to normal." The truth is: "Things aren't going to get back to normal!" Change is now the norm. It is a given. A way of life. To those who believe that "this too shall pass"—sorry! The world isn't going to suddenly stop changing so we can avoid ambiguity and uncertainty. We might as well learn to live with and enjoy life in these changing times.

Technology continues to change at a rapid pace. Today's new products are tomorrow's deals, soon to be no longer in use.

Consider further that a weekday edition of *The New York Times* contains more information than the average person was likely to come across in a lifetime during the seventeenth century in England.

An estimated one hundred scientific research papers will be published today.[2]

My children presented me a musical birthday card on my fortieth birthday. I love gadgets, so I was intrigued every time I opened the card to hear it play "Happy Birthday." For two solid weeks I would test the endurance of this simple toy. I discarded it in the garbage can under the kitchen sink one night before going to bed. The next morning, as I entered the kitchen I heard a faint musical sound. Opening the door below the sink, I couldn't believe my ears. The card's power was dying, but I could faintly hear it playing the programmed tune. Some time later I learned that the three-dollar and fifty cent card contained more computer power than existed in the entire world before 1950.

Today, the watch you are wearing on your wrist contains more computer power than existed in the entire world prior to 1961. In fact, today's cars are powered by more computer technology than *Apollo 11*.

Times have certainly changed. Our lives can be compared to a daily scenario occurring in Africa. Every morning a gazelle wakes up and knows it must run faster today than the fastest lion or be killed. At the same time, a hungry lion realizes it must run faster than the slowest gazelle or go without a delicious meal. The moral: whether a lion or gazelle, when the sun comes up, you'd better be running.

Sound familiar? We run faster and faster every day just to keep up with the harried pace required by life's changing nature. Yet, it seems we can't grow fast enough, learn enough, or adapt quickly enough to meet increasing demands on our time, energy, and mental stamina.

I've learned a couple of things during the road construction and other hasty life-altering changes. First, today is not guaranteed to be a repeat of yesterday. New signs, barricades, and detours pop up without warning. The world is moving too quickly for today to be a repeat of yesterday.

Secondly, the future is not what it used to be. Even the condition of the future changes as quickly as the ticks on the clock. Look back on the past year. You will undoubtedly notice that many events transpired without advance notice or your approval. It seems almost impossible to predict what the future holds in store for us.

The U.S. Census Bureau concluded after a recent survey that, "Change of all types—economic, social, cultural, technological, and political—is occurring at an increasing rate. In some areas, it is not merely accelerating but exploding. The rapid rate of change shows no sign of slowing in our lifetime."[3]

That is a bit unsettling for us habitual types. No doubt about it, we are living in a time of accelerated, unavoidable, unrelenting, unsettling, uncontrollable, nonstop, unnerving change.

However, "Change is growth, both intellectual and emotional," says Dr. Joyce Brothers. "People who are open to change enjoy life far more than those who are bogged down in static status quo."[4]

I've finally concluded that the future belongs to those who not only accept change, but also embrace it, enjoy it, and use it to create their future. It is time to abandon or modify what isn't working anymore. Of course, even the stuff that is good enough today probably won't be good enough tomorrow.

Change dispenses with stability, status quo, and the much beloved comfort zone. People and organizations must learn how to use change and actively participate in it. It is no longer realistic just to cope with change. The choices are to have change forced upon us or to use it to stake our claim in the future. That takes courage!

The twenty-first century challenges to deal with the crucial changes needed to move us forward while maintaining balance in life are immense. It can be done but not without embracing a new revolution.

There are three possible responses to this challenge. There will be those who are on the forefront of the revolution. Others will follow it, and still another group will sleep through it while hoping things will soon get back to normal. The sleepers are in trouble and the followers run the risk of being left in the dust or getting stuck in what the revolutionaries leave behind. Both the sleepers and the followers just keep falling farther behind. As someone once said, "You can't leave footprints in the sands of time if you're sitting on your butt. And, who wants to leave butt prints in the sands of time?"[5]

Don't be too hard on the sleepers and followers, but these sleepers and followers need a wake-up call. Most of what we are taught throughout our early lives is about how to keep things comfortable, secure, and void of undue surprises. It's difficult to forget or to put our lifelong conditioning out of our minds and break the old rules to create new ideas.

Leading a personal revolution requires a recommitment of the mind and heart, along with an enlarged vision of what the future can be. You'll need to fill your tool box with renewed insight and understanding of life's demands. Rethink the present, create new ways of doing things, reinvent present processes, and let go of the past.

It is ludicrous to think anyone can survive, let alone thrive, professionally without a personal transformation that breeds an optimistic, adventurous outlook toward the future. The moment you commit to such a lifestyle, doors of opportunity begin to open. Otherwise, cynicism, pessimism, and fatalism rear their ugly heads. Stress elevates. Desperation levels rise. You disempower yourself. Self-pity reigns.

Facing the rugged terrain of your upcoming journey requires paying a price. Experiencing success in these turbulent times is unlikely without a personal devotion to modify the way we do things. Rather than wasting incredible energy fighting change, holding on to old habits, and resisting new processes, invest your energies in finding ways to align yourself with the changes.

Please realize that if you don't create your future, someone else will. The best way to influence your tomorrow is to make the most of today. The next several chapters offer strategies for maximizing the benefits of change.

> How most of us dread change, fight against it, or, refuse to acknowledge it, even unto the last look in the coffin.
>
> —Gwendolyn Brooks[6]

Chapter 2

GIVE OF YOURSELF

There is no more noble occupation in the world than to assist another human being—to help someone succeed.

Alan Loy McGinnis[1]

HUMANKIND'S REFLEX REACTION TO CHANGE is to focus on *me.* "What's in it for me?" "How will my life be affected?" "Why do all the changes occur in my department?" Such questions become prevalent.

Self-pity parties are scheduled. Human spirits begin to wilt. You begin feeling like the whole world is against you. The devastating effects of change are given permission to take their toll. *Stop.* When was the last time you took an inventory of what you've unselfishly given to others instead of what you thought you should receive from them? How have you given of yourself to someone else this week without expecting anything in return?

I've learned much about this subject from Jimmy Carter. He dreamed of being governor of Georgia and then aspired to the U.S. presidency. His dreams were fulfilled until world events changed.

The Iran hostage crisis erupted and ultimately resulted in a sour end to Carter's presidency. Then what?

Jimmy and Rosalyn dedicated themselves to a new dream of helping the poor through Habitat for Humanity. By building low-cost housing for the poor, the Carters rebounded from disappointment to find excitement and fulfillment in helping others.[2]

Dreams do get demolished. Life can seem unfair. Adversity and calamity surround us. In the midst of it all the natural laws of this universe remain in tact.

One of those laws, the law of reciprocity, indicates that when I help others deal with change, be successful, feel better about life, or work through adversity, my life will be enriched as well. You've heard it before. What you give, you get. What you send out comes back. What you sow, you reap.

Rent the movie *An Officer and a Gentleman*.[3] In it, the hero performs poorly in naval officer training. He is in constant conflict with his superiors. Contrary to military regulations, he shines the shoes of his classmates for money. But, he shines when it comes to performing the obstacle course. It's as if the course were designed for his abilities, and it appears that he has a shot at setting a training record when the class is required to run it for an official time.

The story line really becomes interesting when the soldier's best friend commits suicide and he challenges the noncommissioned officer in charge of his friend's training. He is certain to be kicked out of officer training. However, while his dismissal is pending, his class runs the obstacle course.

One of his classmates is a woman who struggles climbing over one of the obstacles. As the hero pursues an obstacle course record, his classmate becomes stuck on the difficult obstacle. It's the hero's decision-making moment. What should he do? The only thing he had impressed his superiors with was his obstacle course performance. Perhaps if he could set the record, he would not be dismissed from officer training.

Then the unbelievable occurs. The hero stops and rushes back to help his classmate, even though he knows his choice will cost him the record he was destined to set.

This one act of helping someone else results in his superiors allowing him to graduate and become an "officer and a gentleman."

Convincing people in times of change that the best way to increase the quality of their life is do something that will enhance another person's life is difficult. Attention tends to turn inward and gets stuck there. Selfishness takes its ugly seat, and we become occupied with filling our own needs. Just the opposite action is needed to get in tune with what's good for us.

Like an officer and gentleman, we need to reach out unselfishly to help others overcome the obstacles that keep them from being successful. Then, we can experience the benefit of a Peace Corps advertisement: "Feel better about yourself than you ever thought possible."

> We cannot hold a torch to light another's path without brightening our own.
>
> —Ben Sweetland[4]

Chapter 3

COMMIT YOURSELF TO A CHANGE-READY LIFESTYLE

The status quo sets on society like fat on cold chicken soup and it's quite content to be what it is. Unless someone comes along to stir things up there won't be change.

—Abbie Hoffman[1]

I N THE OPENING CHAPTER OF *Tom Sawyer*, Mark Twain shares as interesting conversation that reflects the condition of human nature. Tom tries to persuade his friend Huck to join him in his plans to form a band of robbers and to take captives, much like pirates used to do.

Huck asks Tom what pirates do with the captives they take, and Tom answers, "Ransom them." "Ransom? What's that?" asks Huck. "I don't know. But that's what they do. I seen it in books; and so of course that's what we got to do," explains Tom. "Do you want to go doing different from what's in the books, and get things all muddled up?"[2]

This dialogue represents a way of thinking that's not much different from many people today. It is easier to do what we have always been doing even though the times require us to evaluate, refine, and speed up the things we do. The beliefs of the past shackle us from moving into the future. Unfortunately, like Tom Sawyer, we may not know what we are doing or why, but that's the way it has always been done. So, we blindly follow the traditions of the past.

Instead of attempting to live in a future that is a repeat of yesterday's strategies, abundant opportunities await those who are creative and resilient in these chaotic times. We are designed to encounter life most effectively when we grow at a pace that allows us to stay abreast of the major changes we face. When your life is challenging, but productive and fulfilling, there's evidence you are keeping up with and assimilating the changes you face.

Dean Rusk, former U.S. Secretary of State said, "The pace of events is moving so fast that unless we can find some way to keep our sights on tomorrow, we cannot expect to be in touch with today."[3] The best way to be prepared for an ever-changing tomorrow is to implement a daily growing plan today.

Being change-sensitive, change-ready is not achieved by the snap of your fingers. Overnight express delivery isn't an option. The major challenge is to continually evaluate our thinking. Futurist Faith Popcorn predicted in *The Popcorn Report*: "If you thought it yesterday, if you're thinking it today, you won't think it tomorrow."[4]

To sharpen our thinking and be continually in tune with changing demands, we need to nurture an ongoing attitude that is:

- Open to new ideas
- Willing to explore new techniques and discard worn-out beliefs
- Excited about learning
- Committed to facing challenges and discovering opportunities
- Flexible
- Prepared to leave the past and enter the future

- Constantly prepared to adjust perceptions, practices, and performance

Change agent master Rosabeth Moss Kanter believes, "The individuals who will succeed and flourish will also be masters of change: adept at reorienting their own and others' activities in untried directions to bring about higher levels of achievement. They will be able to acquire and use power to produce innovation."[5]

What habits, limiting beliefs, procedures, attitudes, or self-limiting thoughts are getting in the way? Let them go. As Eddy Ketchursid aptly stated, "If your horse is dead, for goodness sake—dismount!"[6] If you have been doing something a particular way for five or ten years, it's a pretty good sign, in these changing times, that you haven't prepared to master the future. Not to replace them is both professional and personal suicide.

Create a clean sheet today. Decide exactly what you will be doing tomorrow and in the weeks and months to come to keep you on the cutting edge of life's accelerating and complex change.

> He who rejects change is the architect of decay. The only human institution which rejects progress is the cemetery.
>
> —Harold Wilson[7]

Section Two

MAKE THE
BEST OF IT

Chapter 4

DON'T BEAT YOURSELF UP

When you make a mistake, don't look back at it long. Take the reason of the thing into your mind, and then look forward. Mistakes are lessons of wisdom. The past cannot be changed. The future is yet in your power.

—Hugh White[1]

A *PEANUTS* CARTOON FEATURES CHARLIE BROWN reflecting, "Sometimes I lie awake at night and ask, 'Where have I gone wrong?' Then a voice says to me, 'This is going to take more than one night.'"[2]

I can relate to Charlie Brown's personal discovery. If mistakes could be credited toward formal degrees, my walls would be filled with diplomas. At the same time, I agree with Sophia Loren that, "Mistakes are part of the dues one pays for a full life."[3] Although painful at times, a lifetime of mistakes indicates you've lived life to the fullest and have accumulated a collection of valuable experiences.

If you are stretching to improve the quality of your life, mistakes are imminent. You simply cannot step into a world of unknowns and expect to make accurate, perfectly judged decisions. The margin of error is high for people refusing to endorse a life of complacency. If you only rely on past experiences and rehashing old ideas to push you forward, you're going to miss the excitement of expanding your thinking and capturing the adventure of living. In fact, you'll probably find yourself wandering in circles, recycling the same regimen of activities and information. Experimentation lights new fires critical for peak performance.

Coach Paul "Bear" Bryant had a simplistic, yet effective, strategy for dealing with mistakes. He said, "When you make a mistake, there are only three things you should ever do about it: (1) Admit it. (2) Learn from it. (3) Don't repeat it."[4]

Admit your mistakes. The first step is actually admitting you made a mistake. "No man has a chance to enjoy permanent success," asserted Napoleon Hill, "until he begins to look in a mirror for the real cause of all his mistakes."[5] Everyone makes mistakes, and being honest with yourself and others saves energy and speeds up the process for repairing the damages. History teaches that an attempted cover-up will ultimately label you deceptive.

In July of 1994 Intel discovered that its Pentium processing chip had a flaw. Although the chip occasionally computed wrong answers for division problems using large numbers, Intel determined the flaw would only affect the average user once every twenty seven thousand years. Rather than fix or expose the flaw, Intel continued to promote and aggressively sell the defective computer chip.

Within five months, rumors of the flaw spread throughout the computer world. Intel's cover-up was exposed, but they continued to downplay the significance. A dramatic step by IBM to stop selling units with the Pentium chip finally got Intel's attention, and they agreed to exchange the chips when requested. Coming clean ultimately helped the company reclaim their positive image.[6]

Winston Churchill endorsed the belief that, "If you simply take up the attitude of defending a mistake, there will be no hope for improvement."[7] Cover-ups aggravate the mistake. Admission is the beginning point of correction.

Learn from your mistakes. Your blunders, boners, and bloopers are a natural part of life and learning. Life is a trial and error process, and the imperfectness of this process will inevitably produce mistakes. Face it, sometimes the best way to learn the right way of doing things is to first do it the wrong way. Of course, we can't continue doing things the wrong way and just conclude it isn't working.

Dale Carnegie believed, "The successful man will profit from his mistakes and try again in a different way."[8]

The following humorous story was e-mailed to me.

> The weather was very hot, and a man wanted to take a dive in a nearby lake. He didn't bring his swimsuit, but who cared? He was all alone. So he undressed and got into the water.
>
> After some delightful minutes of cool swimming, a pair of old ladies walked onto the shore in his direction. He panicked, got out of the water and grabbed a bucket lying in the sand nearby. He held the bucket in front of his private parts and sighed with relief.
>
> The ladies got nearby and looked at him. He felt awkward and wanted to move. Then one of the ladies said, "You know, I have a special gift, I can read minds."
>
> "Impossible," said the embarrassed man, "you really know what I think?"
>
> "Yes," the lady replied, "right now, I bet you think that the bucket you're holding has a bottom."[9]

Mistakes often expose our feelings, weaknesses, or careless actions. Embarrassment can make it difficult to step back, look at the situation objectively, and determine we will do differently the next time around.

"When I reflect, as I frequently do," Benjamin Franklin pondered, "upon the felicity I have enjoyed, I sometimes say to myself, that were the offer made me, I would engage to run again, from beginning to end, the same career of life. All I would ask, should be the privilege of an author to correct in a second edition, certain errors of the first."[10]

Your "second edition" can begin the second you take responsibility for an error and determine what you have learned to enrich your life. Commit yourself to be big enough to admit your mistakes, smart enough to profit from them, and strong enough to correct them.

Don't repeat your mistakes. Someone once said, "There is nothing wrong with making mistakes. Just don't respond with encores."[11] This is simple, yet profound, advice. Every time we repeat a mistake, the price goes up.

> Two college roommates were enjoying a late night western movie. As they watched a cowboy riding his horse straight toward a cliff, Jim said to his buddy, "I'll bet that guy rides over the cliff."
>
> "He's not dumb enough to do that," Bill responded. "Twenty bucks says you're wrong."
>
> Moments later, the cowboy and his horse headed over the cliff. Bill silently pulled twenty dollars from his billfold and handed it to Jim.
>
> "I can't take your money," Jim responded, "I've seen the movie before."
>
> "So have I," Bill sheepishly said, "but I didn't think the guy would do it again."[12]

Have you ever made a mistake, recognized how stupid it was, and then turned right around and repeated the same mistake? You're not the only one. Repeated blunders are the fruit of habit. Some of our decisions and actions have become second nature, and even failure-laden behaviors are more easily repeated than changed.

Once you break through the cycle of reoccurring mistakes, you create healthier habitual behavior that evolves around making the most of a situation, but you are determined not to repeat it. Pearl Buck suggested, "Every great mistake has a halfway moment, a split second when it can be recalled and perhaps remedied."[13] When you feel yourself beginning to enter the path of a familiar mistake, interrupt the journey, and redirect your efforts.

Don't beat yourself up for messing up, but do admit it, learn from it, and for goodness sake, don't keep repeating it.

> To err is human... but when the eraser wears out ahead of the pencil, you're over doing it.
>
> —Jerry Jenkins[14]

Chapter 5

LIFE CAN BE A BUMMER

Success is not measured by what a man accomplishes, but by
the opposition he has encountered, and the courage with which
he has maintained the struggle against overwhelming odds.

—Charles Lindbergh [1]

A DVERSITY IS A NATURAL PART of life. "Most do not fully see this truth that life is difficult," wrote M. Scott Peck, in *The Road Less Traveled*. "Instead they moan more or less incessantly, noisily or subtly, about the enormity of their problems...as if life were generally easy, as if life *should* be easy." Life isn't easy. Life can be blatantly tough. Difficulties are as much a natural part of life as the air we breathe. Like it or not, trials and tribulations come with the territory of living. It's all a part of living in an imperfect world.

To ignore the fact that the continual presence of adversity also applies to work would indicate the ultimate in self-deception. You'll frequently find yourself in the middle of painful situations, perplexities, and problems, or waiting for them to reveal their ugly heads.

One thing is for sure: these situations will reveal the substance of which you're really made.

Setbacks sting. They can knock you off your feet or cause you to step back, evaluate your situation, and determine what you can learn. Victory comes when you accept the fact that the challenges, difficulties, and sometimes heartbreaking disappointments you experience need not ruin your life. Walt Disney once reflected, "All the adversity I've had in my life, all my troubles and obstacles have strengthened me . . . you may not realize it when it happens, but a kick in the teeth may be the best thing in the world for you."[3] It will probably take some considerable convincing to get us to that way of thinking. Taking small, incremental steps in that direction is a start.

Every day, multitudes of people count themselves victors over unfortunate, and sometimes seemingly unbearable, challenges. Rather than protest the inequities of their situation, which seems to be popular today, they adjust their attitudes, harness their energies, and elevate themselves to perform at a higher level. In many cases, they go on to perform far above the expected results.

Let me refresh your memory concerning a few of these people. In spite of having his first novel (*A Time to Kill*) rejected by twenty-eight publishers, John Grisham has sold millions of copies of such books as *The Firm* and *The Client*. It takes incredible fortitude to keep on writing when twenty-eight people have indicated they don't think much of your work. Now, every time he turns out another new book, newspapers, book reviewers, and movie producers take notice. It is common to see Grisham's name and book titles listed on the nation's best-seller lists.[4] Grisham would probably agree with Harry Emerson Fosdick, who said: "Life does not simply ask, how much can you do? It asks how much you can endure, and still be unspoiled? What a testing of character adversity is!"[5]

Jane Pauley would concur. Being a six-time loser in the Homecoming Queen elections in school didn't keep Jane Pauley from becoming a famous television personality. Then, at the top of a seemingly perfect career, she was encouraged to make a much publicized exit from national prominence.[6] Enough is enough...right? Not for Jane Pauley. She stepped back, refocused, and went on to help create an award winning news show that, once again, allowed her to excel in front of the camera.

"Show me someone who has done something worthwhile," said Lou Holtz, "and I'll show you someone who has overcome adversity."[7] Diving champion Greg Louganis is a good example of that. He was in first place in the springboard diving preliminaries at the 1988 Summer Olympics when he hit his head on the ninth dive. Even stitches couldn't blur his focus. Instead of hanging up his trunks, Louganis maintained his concentration and executed one of the best dives of the competition.[8] Adversity causes some people to lie down and quit, while it inspires others to reach new levels. "Adversity causes some men to break; others to break records," declared William Arthur Ward.[9]

Franklin D. Roosevelt was paralyzed by polio at the age of thirty-nine but didn't let the pain and disability keep him from pursuing his potential. Eight years later, he became governor of New York, and in 1932 he was elected president of the United States.[10] Steve Palermo's successful career as an American League umpire was interrupted when he was shot coming to the aid of a robbery victim. After hundreds of hours of rehabilitation, he regained partial use of his legs and reemerged in baseball as the special assistant to the chairman of Major League Baseball's governing Executive Council.[11] Woody Allen flunked motion picture production at New York University and the City College of New York. Even failing English didn't keep Allen from becoming an Academy Award-winning writer, producer, and director.[12]

These men, representing diverse backgrounds and experiences, share a common bond. Life wasn't kind. Some bad things just happen (like polio), other bad things are done to us (like being shot) and some bad things can be the result of our own frailties (like flunking classes). No matter what the situation, Napoleon Hill was right. "Life is a struggle," he said, "and the rewards go to those who meet difficulty face-to-face, overcome it, and move on to the next challenge."[13]

Robert Schuller suggested that, "Most people who succeed in the face of seemingly impossible conditions are people who simply don't know how to quit."[14]

Lee Iacocca was on the top of his career in 1978. Iacocca had just orchestrated two record years of profit for Ford Motor Company when Henry Ford called Iacocca into his office and fired him. Within two weeks, after ending his thirty-two-year career with Ford, Iacocca took over control of the struggling, almost bankrupt, Chrysler Corporation. In addition to dealing with being fired, he now faced a tremendous challenge to keep Chrysler alive. Iacocca pulled out all the stops, begged the government for a loan, agreed to forego a personal salary, walked the manufacturing floors to keep hope alive, and turned a major personal letdown and pending corporate tragedy into his greatest opportunity.[15]

Vanessa Williams was forced to resign in 1984 as the first black Miss America because of a mistake she made as a teenager in posing for nude photos. One thing led to another. She was turned down by a co-op apartment board in New York City as an "inappropriate person." Her audition for the Broadway musical *My One and Only* was vetoed by the powers that be. Williams persisted and made her mark as a singer with several Grammy Award nominations and landed a highly applauded starring role in *Kiss of the Spider Woman*.[16]

Looking back on her hard knocks, Ms. Williams could surely relate to the words of Samuel Johnson when he said, "Life affords no higher pleasure than that of surmounting difficulties, passing from one step of success to another, forming new wishes and seeing them gratified."[17]

When we look at all the achievers mentioned and their incredible tenacity, we should draw courage and comfort from their experiences. Their stubborn refusal to allow adversity to darken their lives is a testament to our ability to deal with life's less than pleasurable circumstances. "History has demonstrated," observed publisher B.C. Forbes, "that the most notable winners usually encountered heartbreaking obstacles before they triumphed. They won because they refused to become discouraged by their defeats."[18]

Maybe you have felt like the humorist who said, "When I was feeling down, someone told me, 'Cheer up, things could get worse.' So I cheered up—and they did!"[19] "When things are bad, we take a bit of comfort in the thought that they could be worse," Malcolm Forbes comforted. "And when they are, we find hope in the thought that things are so bad they have to get better."[20]

Take heart. The valleys of your career are inevitable. They are also unpredictable. We rarely know what challenge lurks around the corner. Life is simply a mixture of pleasure and pain, intended to produce maturity.

Adversity is not a respecter of persons. It is totally impartial. When you experience a downturn in life, it doesn't mean you are a bad person. You're human. Don't ask, "Why me?" A more suitable response is, "Why not me?" William James believed, "Acceptance of what has happened is the first step to overcoming the consequences of any misfortune."[21]

Your disappointing times are temporary. They won't last forever and, in light of your entire career, they are short-lived. For these brief moments, there is a purpose to the pain. Henry Ward Beecher believed, "Troubles are often the tools by which God fashions us for better things."[22] Every difficulty possesses the opportunity for us to change, grow, and build character. Each experience is a natural part of the process of shaping and molding the person you can become and preparing the way for the career success you can experience. God doesn't cause bad things to happen, but He uses them to build us.

Stedham Graham suggested, "There are two ways to respond when your vision for a better life is challenged. You either give up or step up."[23] When faced with undesirable situations, you can "step up" by:

1. Knowing exactly what you face. Get the facts.
2. Determining the worst possible outcome and how you would deal with it.
3. Determining what advantageous purpose this difficulty can serve.
4. Using the situation to gain new insights about yourself and forming strategies for dealing with the challenge.
5. Beginning to take action that will prepare you for the worst possible outcome.
6. Refusing to feel sorry for yourself.
7. Accepting full responsibility for your response.
8. Working with an unwavering spirit to meet the challenge head-on.
9. Continually focusing on how you will grow from this situation.
10. Acknowledging all of the good things in your life.

You can navigate your way through the adversities of life and refuse to give in to the impulse to quit. There will be times when your dreams are crushed and your hopes become clouded. You might feel like an utter failure or begin to question your competence. Doubt can set in, making you wonder if things will ever get better.

Norman Vincent Peale endured his fair share of adversity and yet surfaced stronger and more positive each time. He wrote in *Enthusiasm Makes the Difference*:

> Without struggle, how could a person become rounded and mature and strong?...Not only are trouble and suffering inevitable, but they serve a definite creative purpose...You gradually learn to take difficulties as part of the maturing process. So when the going gets tough, take the attitude that rough spots are being knocked off. That you are being shaped for the real purpose of your life...As tough and unpleasant as difficulty may be, it is the source of potential development.[24]

The impact adversity has on your life is up to you:

> The important and decisive factor in life is not what happens to us, but the attitude we take toward what happens. The surest revelation of one's character is the way one bears one's suffering. Circumstances and situations may color life, but by the grace of God, we have been given the power to choose what that color shall be. The effect that misfortune, handicap, sickness, and sorrow have upon life is determined by the way in which we meet them.
>
> —Charles R. Woodson[25]

Chapter 6

Escape the Bottom of the Can

We must look for ways to be an active force in our own lives.
We must take charge of our own destinies, design a life of
substance, and truly begin to live our dreams.

—Les Brown[1]

I WAS SCHEDULED TO CONDUCT AN all day program entitled,
"Bringing Out the Best in You" at a community college. This
motivational, personal development seminar was offered
to all students. I arrived early in the morning to get set up and
mentally prepare for the day. Then, I experienced the ultimate ego-
buster...nobody came. That's right, not one person showed up, and
to top it off, the seminar organizer wasn't surprised. "Even though
we offer to pay students to come," he said, "they don't see the benefit
in participating."

"Help me understand," I said, showing my disbelief.

"Do you fish?" my host asked.

"Only if I have to," I responded as we both chuckled.

Then he turned serious. "Imagine two fishers, sitting on a river-
bank next to each other, enjoying the warmth of the day and their

favorite leisure activity. One fisherman is struggling to keep his crab bait in the can. The crabs keep climbing up the side of the can, and the fisherman pushes them back down. He notices his fishing buddy doesn't have a problem with his bait. The crab all sit motionless at the bottom of the can."

"How do you keep your bait from escaping?" the fisherman asked his partner.

"It's very simple," the man replied. "I have one crab who loves the bottom of the can and is offended when others try to escape. When that happens, he reaches up and pulls them back to the bottom. Eventually, they all become satisfied with their condition at the bottom of the can."

"That's a powerful story!" I said.

"It's more than a story," he immediately responded. "It's a way of life."

I stared out the windshield of my rental car on the trip back to the airport. "It's a way of life," kept ringing in my ears. That explained the continued high unemployment rate, frequency of alcoholism, history of self-destructive behavior; not to mention a lack of interest in attending a personal development program. No matter how hard someone tried to escape, the pull to remain at the bottom of the can prevailed.

Every culture, society, community, and organization has a "bottom of the can" population who threaten to spread an epidemic of despair. The "bottom of the can" insulates people from the real world, with a false sense of security, comfort, and protection from the realities of the outside world. They remain isolated from the world's vast opportunities, richness of life and the potential for something better by proclaiming themselves victims. Their escape is prolonged, if not averted altogether, by their unwillingness to move from passive victims to active achievers. Ultimately, their deceptive maneuvers strip them and those around them of positive life choices, attitudes, and actions.

When we learn to despise the "bottom of the can" mentality, we set the wheels in motion to escape destructive habits, emotional trauma, relational discourse, and the victim mentality. "The moment the slave resolves that he will no longer be a slave, his fetters fall," believed Indian nationalist and spiritual leader Mohandas Gandhi. "He frees himself and shows the way to others. Freedom and slavery are mental states."[2] I love this final comment about freedom and slavery being mental states. Both are choices. Living at the bottom of the can is a choice.

I encourage you to live an empowered life, where you hold yourself accountable for escaping self-made prisons of misery by resisting the pull of toxic people and environments. Dr. Benjamin Elijah Mays, former president of Morehouse College, said, "It is not your environment, it is you —the quality of your mind, the integrity of your soul, the determination of your will—that will decide your future and shape your life."[3] Don't count on anyone else coming along to pull you out. Put yourself in charge of escape. You are the one who must see and endorse the future benefits of this self-determined lifestyle, or the motivation to take charge of your life will be lost.

The journey up the side of the can begins with you. Take the initiative. Make the first move. Climb deliberately, expecting a tug to return to the bottom. Resist. Ignore those who try to discourage you. Don't give up and don't give in. This bold move takes courage, but the view and experience on the outside is well worth the effort.

> On the river of life are strong currents which, left unchallenged, carry us downstream. We can either choose to be their passive victim, or we can start actively going against the flow.
> —Kurt D. Bruner[4]

Chapter 7

Be Better than Average

Always dream and shoot higher than you know you can do.
Don't bother just to be better than your contemporaries or
predecessors. Try to be better than yourself.

—William Faulkner[1]

FROM THE INSPIRING PEN OF the Nobel Prize-winning
novelist William Faulkner to the following challenges from
an unknown author, we are encouraged to reach beyond
where we are and move toward our potential.

"Average" is what the failures lay claim to when their family
and friends ask them why they are not successful.

"Average" is the top of the bottom, the best of the worst, the
bottom of the top, the worst of the best. Which of these are you?

"Average" means being run-of-the-mill, mediocre, insignifi-
cant, a nonentity.

Being "average" is the lazy person's cop out; it's lacking the
guts to stand in life; it's living by default.

Being "average" is to take up space for purpose, to take the trip through life, but to never pay the fare, to return interest for God's investment in you.

Being "average" is to pass one's life away with time, rather than to pass one's time away with life. It's to kill time, rather than work it to death.

To be "average" is to be forgotten once you pass this life. The successful are remembered for their contributions, the failures are remembered because they tried, but the "average," the silent majority, are just forgotten.

To be "average" is to commit the greatest crime one can against one's self, humanity, and one's God. The saddest epitaph is this: "Here lie Mr. and Mrs. Average—here lies the remains of what might have been, except for their belief that they were only 'average'."

—Edmund Gaudet[2]

Jane Wagner, writing in her book *The Search for Signs of Intelligent Life in the Universe* had this provocative observation: "I worry that our lives are like soap operas. We can go for months and not tune in to them, then six months later we look in and the same stuff is still going on."[3] What a sad but accurate reflection of the "average" lifestyle.

Phillips Brooks said,

Dreadful will be the day when the world becomes contented, when one great universal satisfaction spreads itself over the world. Sad will be the day for every man when he becomes absolutely contented with the life that he is living, with the thoughts that he is thinking, with the deeds that he is doing, when there is not forever beating at the doors of his soul some great desire to do something larger which he knows that he was meant and made to do because he is a child of God.[4]

What thoughts do you need to challenge? On what deeds could you raise the level of performance? Where have you become content in life, knowing that there is so much more to experience? What is your present desire quotient?

Put a dose of life into your living by refusing to be content with the average. Whatever your plans are today, whatever activities you indulge in, whatever responsibilities are passed on to you, whatever challenges you encounter, don't let the day go by without trying to improve yourself in some way. Leave the comfort of "average" and pursue the elation of excellence. Pay the price to reach toward your potential.

> Over and over again mediocrity is promoted because real worth isn't to be found.
>
> — Kathleen Norris[5]

Section Three

REMEMBER, IT COULD BE WORSE

Chapter 8

LEARN TO EXPECT
(AND ENJOY) THE UNEXPECTED

If life were predictable, it would cease to be life and would be without flavor.

—Eleanor Roosevelt[1]

HAVE YOU EVER NOTICED HOW profound the *Peanuts* cartoon can be? I love the one where Charlie Brown, in the first panel, says,

"I learned something in school today. I signed up for folk guitar, computer programming, stained glass, art, shoemaking, and a natural foods workshop."

The second panel has him saying, "I got spelling, history, arithmetic, and two study periods."

The third panel has his companion asking, "So, what did you learn?"

Charlie Brown offers a practical life lesson in the final panel. "I learned that what you sign up for and what you get are two different things."[2]

How many times have you heard someone say, "Life isn't fair. I signed up for success, happiness, and fulfillment, and I got challenges, disappointment, and failure. It's just not fair!"

Life is unpredictable. There is no short-order cook at our beck and call to ensure everything we order is served just as we like it. Sometimes we take what's been served and make the most of it. As someone once said, "The real enjoyment of living, like the real enjoyment of eating a steak, comes when you put your teeth into it."[3]

If life is going to be unpredictable, then what can we do about it? Good question. Some people just give up. They entertain the attitude that "What will be, will be," thereby eliminating any effort to change or mold what's happening to them. Resigning yourself to the belief that there's nothing you can do to improve your life is certainly not advisable.

How about altering your expectations? The reality is that some people have a tendency to expect life to bring them whatever they want, when they want it. Those who are willing to adjust this thinking endorse the insight of Kathleen Norris that, "Life is easier to take than you'd think: All that is necessary is to accept the impossible, do without the indispensable, and bear the intolerables."[4]

I'm partial to another alternative. Madeleine L'Engle said, "When we stop waking up in the morning as though each day was going to be full of adventure, joys, and dangers, and wake up instead to the alarm clock and the daily grind, and mutter about TGIF, we lose the newborn quality of belief which is so lovely in a child."[5] Approach the unpredictable with wonderment. Sustain the child-like curiosity and fascination with everything you encounter. Expect the unexpected. Enjoy it.

This approach runs contrary to public opinion. The majority of us would agree with George Gissing, writing in *The Private Papers of Henry Ryecroft*. He asserted: "It is familiarity with life that makes time speed quickly. When every day is a step in the unknown—as for children—the days are long with gathering of experience."[6]

He might be right, but consider this: By increasing our exposure to the unfamiliar, we increase our repertoire of the familiar. How can we ever increase our comfort with the unfamiliar unless we increase our exposure to the uncomfortable? Those who lay down and surrender, run or fight that which bothers them, will live in a continual state of anxiety. Limited experiences create a limited life. If you want to expand the quality of your life, put out the welcome mat for unexpected visitors, and enjoy their visit. "Whatever the ups and downs of detail within our limited experience," said Gregory Bateson, "the larger whole is primarily beautiful."[7] That's true, unless, of course, we decide to lament the ups and downs while failing to enjoy the larger whole.

If you are waiting to live life until everything happens the way you want it to—good luck.

Develop an increased tolerance for unpredictable events to interrupt your master plan, to modify your course direction, and to spring surprises your way. Give an accepting nod to increased confusion and seemingly pointless changes. We can always use what life has to offer by proactively pursuing the stockpile of possibilities. Think of your life as having movable walls that adjust to fit current demands rather than fixed walls that fracture when pressured.

Life is not predictable, in the sense that it brings you whatever you want, whenever you want it. But to those willing to expand the dimensions of their living, life will predictably produce unanticipated experiences to add richness to your living.

> You have to look at each day as a new opportunity to change one thing about your life.
>
> —Rick Pitino[8]

Chapter 9

HANG ON THROUGH TURBULENT TIMES

Life is a series of problems. To confront them is often painful;
yet it is only through solving problems that we grow... and give
meaning to our lives. Many of us try to avoid our problems and
the emotional suffering they involve, and this tendency is the
primary basis of all mental illness.

—paraphrase of M. Scott Peck, M.D.[1]

I HESITATE TO OVER-PROMOTE THE BENEFITS of adversity, but
here's an observation worth your reflection. Problems produce
miracles. It's true. Countless people endured more than they
ever thought possible. Others in difficult situations encounter
unexpected benefits. Renewed strength is experienced through the
process of encouragement and working through daily challenges.

A life without difficulties, like earth exposed to constant sunshine
without rain, becomes a barren desert. A life mixed with pleasure
and pain produces miracles and maturity. Life needs both good and
bad to be purposeful. If you're presently enduring a difficult time,
prepare for a miracle.

Problems are also a primary source for discovering opportunity. Every form of trial reveals needs, and needs sensitize us to previously unexposed opportunities. Don't overlook them by being distracted with the problem or deceived by the seemingly insurmountable consequences. Rather, fine tune your vision. Problems are only opportunities disguised by discomfort.

As I observe people from all walks of life, one conclusion is easily made. The difference between an overwhelming problem and an opportunity is simply the person's perception of the situation. As philosopher Mafu so aptly stated, "If one's primary focus is on the manure pile, he or she will ultimately turn over flowers that 'get in the way' because one is only looking for the manure."[2]

On a recent visit to the South, I learned that years ago farmers in southern Alabama were accustomed to planting one crop every year: cotton. They would plow as much ground as they could and plant their crop. Year after year, they thrived on cotton.

Then one year the dreaded boll weevil devastated the whole area. The next year the farmers, intent on maintaining their livelihood, mortgaged their homes and planted cotton again, hoping for a good harvest. But as the cotton began to grow, the insects returned, infesting and destroying the crop, wiping out most of the farms.

The few who survived those two years of the boll weevil decided to experiment the third year, so they planted something they'd never planted before—peanuts. Peanuts proved hardy, and a wide open market proved so profitable that the farmers who survived the first two years reaped income that third year that enabled them to pay off all their debts. Peanuts became the crop of choice, and farmers prospered with the product of adversity.

Then you know what those farmers did? They spent some of their new wealth to erect in the town square a monument to the boll weevil. The inscription of the monument reads: "In profound appreciation of the boll weevil and what it has done to herald prosperity."[3] If it hadn't been for the boll weevil, they never would have discovered peanuts. They learned that out of disaster, a new profitable opportunity could be discovered.

Inside of every problem is an opportunity waiting to be discovered. Once the blinders of blaming, defensiveness, negative attitudes, and self-pity are removed, intimidating situations can unveil positive solutions.

I'm not suggesting we ignore our problems. Quite the contrary. Face them head on. Be honest about the possible ramifications. See the circumstances as they really are—just circumstances. Face up to the tendency to respond negatively and dispel all temptation to dwell on the negative. Get a grip on your feelings and act in a way that will propel you toward discovering all the good that can result from your present situation.

I was recently told about a commuter flight from Portland, Maine, to Boston. During this uneventful flight, Henry Dempsey, the pilot, suddenly heard an unusual noise coming from the rear of the aircraft. He turned over the controls of the aircraft to his co-pilot and made his way to the back to check out the mysterious sound.

As he reached the tail section, the plane encountered an air pocket and Dempsey was thrust against the rear door. He quickly discovered the reason for the mysterious noise. The rear door was inadvertently left partially unlatched prior to take-off. The door flew open, and Dempsey was sucked from the airplane's cabin out of the jet.

The co-pilot immediately saw the red light indicating an open door. He radioed the nearest airport informing them of his dilemma and requested an emergency landing. He told the air traffic controller that the pilot had fallen out of the plane and requested that emergency personnel search the ocean below.

After the plane landed, Henry Dempsey was found holding onto the ladder of the aircraft. He had miraculously caught the ladder, held on for ten minutes as the plane flew two hundred mph at an altitude of four thousand feet, and then during the landing, kept his head from hitting the runway only twelve inches below. Once safely on the ground, it took airport personnel several minutes to pry Dempsey from the ladder.

Holding on can be difficult when times are tough. In fact, you might have experienced turbulence when letting go and giving up seemed the easiest thing to do. Winners are the people who keep on keeping on when the easy way out would be to get off. Henry Dempsey is proof that the best approach is to hang on for dear life until safety is reached.[4]

The next time life deals you a nasty blow, your dreams go up in smoke, or unexpected tragedy strikes, it's time to push the reset button. Make new plans. Dream new dreams. Resist the temptation to run away, hide, give up, or cash it in. You are in line to make amazing discoveries about yourself and life. Propel yourself forward by establishing positive and fresh expectations.

I can assure you there will be turbulence ahead. Adversity is a given. Disappointment is a normal experience. But, defeat need not be the end result. You have at your disposal the intestinal fortitude to hang on until a safe landing can be maneuvered.

> When things are bad we take a bit of comfort in the thought that they could be worse. And when they are, we find hope in the thought that things are so bad they have to get better.
> —Malcolm Forbes[5]

Chapter 10

RECOGNIZE THE VALUE OF CATFISH

Women [people] are like tea bags. You never know how strong
they are until they're in hot water.

—Eleanor Roosevelt[1]

WHILE IN THE WILDERNESS, JESUS was clearly tempted by Satan to misuse His power. When Satan said, "Worship me, and You will own the world," Jesus said, "No thanks." Then Satan used a little different approach, "Satisfy Your hunger, and turn these stones into bread." Again, Jesus calmly replied, "No."

"Throw yourself off the pinnacle of the temple," Satan tempted, "and test your power to spring back to eternal life." Jesus looked Satan square in the face and said, "No." (Sometimes I think Jesus should have asked Satan, "What part of *no* don't you understand?")

Anyway, after forty days of being tested in that desert, Jesus emerged with a renewed understanding of who He was and what His purpose was.[2]

Adversity tends to reveal our true character. William Penn saw it this way, "No pain, no palm; no thorns, no throne; no gall, no glory;

no cross, no crown."[3] The refining process of adversity prepares us for the victories to follow.

Charles Swindoll uses a story about codfish to simplify this principle. Codfish became a popular choice of many New Englanders, and the demand for cod spread nationwide. A problem occurred when shipping the fish throughout the country. At first, the transport companies tried freezing the cod, but freezing diminished the flavor of the fish. Secondly, they tried shipping the codfish alive in tanks of seawater, but they too lost their flavor and also became soft and mushy.

Then an original thinker offered a clever solution. The codfish were placed in seawater with their natural enemy, the catfish. Imagine this picture. During shipment the catfish chased the cod around the tank—a little game of tag if you will. And when the fish arrived at their destination, the cod were as fresh as those consumed by New Englanders. There was no loss of flavor or texture.[4]

Imagine the adversity in your life created by the "catfish" who were appointed to keep you fresh, active, growing. They help keep you in a continual process of perfecting your character. Then we, like Jesus, when emerging from the desert, can declare "I Am."[5]

Eleanor Roosevelt once said about encountering adversity: "You gain strength, courage, and confidence by every experience in which you really stop to look fear in the face. You are able to say to yourself, 'I've lived through this horror. I can take the next thing that comes along'... You must do the thing you think you cannot do."[6]

I don't necessarily care for the "catfish" in my life but I'm beginning to appreciate their purpose and significance.

Life does not have to be perfect to be wonderful.

—Annette Funicello[7]

Chapter 11

BREAK THROUGH THE BRICK WALL OF ADVERSITY

Success is not measured by what a man accomplishes, but by the opposition he has encountered, and the courage with which he has maintained the struggle against overwhelming odds.

—Charles Lindbergh[1]

SHE HELD THE AUDIENCE IN the palm of her hand. Two thousand people were captivated by her vibrant personality, distinguished stage presence, and the power of her message. Hardly an eye focused on the wheelchair or the disability that made it necessary. All eyes, ears, and hearts were endeared by the person and her challenge to capitalize on our God-given abilities even though our disabilities are more easily spotted.

Joni Eareckson Tada was paralyzed from the shoulders down as a result of a diving accident at the age of seventeen. Through the struggles that ensued, Joni was led to allow God to use her adversity to minister to others with disabilities and their families.

Joni is an internationally recognized artist (which she accomplished by holding a brush or pencil in her mouth), author, lecturer, and musician. Her ministry and talents have helped the world to understand that disabilities are merely challenges to be met and mastered with the grace of God.[2]

"We can decide to let our trials crush us," wrote Helen Keller, "or we can convert them to new forces of good."[3]

Joni's new forces of good have extended throughout the world. She epitomizes one who learned to transform a physical adversity into a blessing and challenge for all those who encounter her talents.

Facing our difficulties head on can be the springboard for building personal effectiveness. As Joni found, without her disability she might never have found her deeper talents. She decided to use them rather than succumb to the adversity she encountered.

Dr. Michael LeBoeuf believes, "Adversity is an experience, not a final act."[4]

On the last day of the 1979 spring baseball exhibition season, Steve Kemp, left-fielder for the Detroit Tigers, took a pitch to the head and was rushed to the hospital.

Would this feared event minimize Kemp's effectiveness at the plate? Would the nightmare of that disastrous pitch haunt him at every at bat? Only time would tell.

On opening day of the regular season, Kemp stepped to the plate with confidence. His first at bat yielded a single, and a home run followed at his next time at bat. The questions had been answered.

During a post-game interview Kemp commented, "After I was hit, I just told myself, 'I can't let it bother me...If you let it bother you, you're not going to be any good to yourself or your team.'"[5]

The brick wall of adversity blocks the road to achievement when viewed as an unconquerable barrier with life-long consequences. Nothing can be further from the truth. A tragedy can be transformed into a triumph when viewed as a temporary roadblock—not a permanent condition.

It could be said that only those who persist through challenges can expect to rise to new heights. Mountains are designed to spur us on to loftier heights.

Bible teacher Warren Wiersbe tells the story of a little boy who was leading his younger sister up a steep mountain path. The climbing was difficult since there were many rocks in the way. Finally, the little girl, exasperated by the hard climb, said to her brother, "This isn't a path at all. It's all rocky and bumpy." "Sure," her brother replied, "but the bumps are what you climb on."[6]

In his book *Enthusiasm Makes the Difference*, Norman Vincent Peale offers encouraging words paraphrased here:

> Without struggle, how could a person become rounded and mature and strong? Not only are trouble and suffering inevitable, but they serve a definite creative purpose. You gradually learn to take difficulties as part of the maturing process. So when the going gets tough, take the attitude that rough spots are being knocked off. That you are being shaped for the real purpose of your life. As tough and unpleasant as difficulty may be, it is the source of potential development.[7]

A life void of difficulties would reduce all possibilities to zero. Eliminate challenges, and the tension needed to produce would be non-existent. We all have a tendency to want to eliminate problems, but they await our willingness to conquer.

Life can be a struggle. The rewards are reserved for those who meet difficulties head on, work through and overcome them, and then move on to the next challenge. Through it all comes this realization: Success is achieved only through struggle. There is no shortcut. The worthwhile achievements in your life are the result of courageously negotiating struggles. You'll become only as big as the problem that stops you.

> You gotta play the hand that's dealt you. There may be pain in that hand, but you play it. And I've played it.
> —James Brady[8]

Section Four

DE-STRESS YOUR STRESS

Chapter 12

HOW TO KEEP FROM BEING WIRED AND TIRED

Life is reduced to work, tasks, effort, an endless list of shoulds and musts...minus the necessary fun and laughter that keeps everything in perspective.

—Charles Swindoll[1]

FOR TOO MANY PEOPLE, THE stresses of life have zapped their ability to do their best, be their best, and enjoy their daily activities.

We can learn a marvelous lesson from the tight-wire aerialist. Each of her moves is made with precision and mastery, yet the casual observer may not recognize the key components for successful performance.

The aerialist focuses primarily on maintaining balance. Every step is orchestrated by carefully touching her toes to the wire and keeping her eyes firmly planted on her goal.

Balance and focus are necessary to capitalize on the productive elements of stress and avoid being overwhelmed by negative stress.

Stress Management Strategies

1. Get in the driver's seat. Emotionally healthy people tend to maintain a high degree of control over what happens in their lives. Feeling in-control helps reduce feelings of stress. You may not be able to control life's events, people's demands, or pressures on the job, but you can decide how to respond to these situations.

2. Passionately pursue your purpose. An article in *Success* magazine noted, "Those who feel a sense of purpose and commitment, who view change as a challenge instead of a threat, aren't affected by stress in a negative way."[2] A personal mission adds direction, meaning, and an empowering element during stressful times. Without purpose, stressful events throw us out of balance.

3. Work your plan. Take one thing at a time. Refrain from procrastinating. Complete uncompleted tasks. Choose how you spend your time. Determine your priorities, and make sure they are built into your weekly schedule.

4. Put problems in perspective. Michael LeBoeuf believes, "Most stress is caused by people who overestimate the importance of their problems."[3] Problems are unfortunate, but most are not catastrophic. Use your talents, abilities, strengths, and energy to make the best of those difficult situations. Break problems down into manageable pieces, and go to work on resolution.

5. Become a kookaburra. A what? Kookaburras are Australian birds known for their deep laughing sound. When was the last time you had a good, belly-wrenching laugh? Pre-schoolers laugh an estimated four hundred fifty times a day; adults laugh only fifteen times a day. Who leads a more relaxed and healthy life? Everytime we laugh, we lower our stress levels.

6. Don't strangle yourself. *Worry* comes from Anglo-Saxon, meaning "to strangle or choke."[4] Worry restricts your ability to think and act effectively. The best cure I know for worry is action. When we take action against something we are worried about, the unnecessary strangling effects of worry begin to lose their hold.

Emerson put it this way: "Do the thing you fear the most, and the death of fear is certain."[5]

7. Listen to what you are saying. Our self-talk and perceptions of events cause undue stress. We become what we think, and our perception of any event will determine our reaction to it. Never underestimate the power of the habitual thoughts, expectations, and beliefs you hold in your mind.

8. Are we having fun yet? Fun is a diversion from the norm that gets us out of the rut the stressors of life create. So when was the last time you escaped the rut and had good, clean fun?

9. Build a buddy system. Focus on building quality relationships. Give up judging, criticizing, holding grudges, unnecessary competition, and the like. Earn your neighbor's love, say something nice to everyone you meet, help someone with one of their problems.

10. Change your oil. Most people take better care of their cars than they do themselves. To keep your body well tuned, learn to relax, take a recess, exercise, build an energy reserve through smart nutrition, recognize your limits, eliminate perfectionism and unrealistic expectations, and release emotions by talking with good friends.

11. See streams in the desert. Keep life in perspective. Concentrate on the positive. Approach failures and mistakes as opportunities. Develop and nurture your enthusiasm. See something good in every experience you have. Persevere in difficult times because better days are ahead. Every day is a new day.

> Stress is an inside job! It's caused by what happens between your ears, by how you look at, think about, and respond to events.
>
> —John Newman[6]

Chapter 13

A PRIMER ON MASTERING STRESS

The most frequent causes of stress are an inability to adapt and not having an established code of behavior to guide our actions.
—Dr. Hans Selye[1]

STRESS IS A USED, MISUSED, abused, and overused word in our daily conversations. What really is stress?

Dr. Hans Selye, the father of stress management research, says, "Stress is the wear and tear on your body caused by life's events."[2] It is the body's physical, mental, and chemical reactions to circumstances that frighten, excite, confuse, endanger, and irritate.

Hundreds of experiences in life cause stress. These stressors create eustress (good stress) or distress (negative stress). Our bodies are designed to meet these stressors. However, each person must determine what is the right amount of stress at his or her optimum level.

Experiencing too little stress causes irritability, boredom, dullness, and apathy. Too much stress can produce comparable results, along with feelings of being overwhelmed.

Dr. Seyle believed the most frequent causes of stress are an inability to adapt and not having an established code of behavior to guide our actions.

Adapt? This planet was once populated by dinosaurs the size of which we have not seen since on this earth. Then something happened. Within a relatively short period of time, virtually all of the beasts vanished.

Dinosaurs, with their inability to adapt to a changing world, became extinct.

Another creature lived during the dinosaur age. That species remains in existence today because of their ability to adapt. Frogs. Yes, those amphibious, adaptable creatures survived the changes.

Before we get too gung-ho about adapting, don't forget the second cause of stress...not having an established code of behavior to guide our actions.

In a laboratory experiment, frogs were placed in a shallow pan of room temperature water. They were free to jump out of the pan at will. Under each pan was a Bunsen burner, which heated the water very gradually. As the temperature rose, the frogs adapted. Unfortunately, regardless of how hot the water became, the frogs never became uncomfortable enough to jump out of the pan.

So what happened? The frogs died because they did not have a code of behavior that told them to jump.

Likewise, we need to learn when enough is enough. Adapting is fine but not without a code of behavior that warns us when it is time to jump. That same code is a warning signal that lets us know it is time to take action to deal with the stressors that now threaten our healthy existence.

Dr. Paul Rosch at the American Institute of Stress says, "The answer to stress management is to realize that stress is an unavoidable consequence of life."[3] Stress is a given in life, but the impact on us is determined by how we respond to the experiences that cause stress.

Dealing with stress is an inside job. Adapt to it, learn from it, and enjoy the positive results it can produce, but beware of getting burned by it.

> I am so tired, and I am crabby. There are enough nights when my husband and I are reduced to eating cheese rinds and tuna fish out of the can because we don't have anything in the refrigerator. I can't get the energy to cook, and I think, "I'm going to lose this man over a tuna sandwich."
>
> —Candice Bergen[4]

Chapter 14

SURVIVAL OF THE STRESSED

Some days you tame the tiger. And some days the tiger has you for lunch.

—Tug McGraw[1]

ACCORDING TO CNN, 28 PERCENT of the American work force voluntarily took pay cuts in 1998 to have more free time, less stress, and more balance in their lives.[2]

The Associated Press recently reported the ulcer drug Prilosec® became the pharmaceutical industry's first $5 billion prescription medication. Prilosec® beat out the number two cholesterol drug Zolor® by $1.1 billion and the highly publicized Viagra® by over $4 billion.[3]

A study by the National Mental Health Association revealed the costs of depression in the workplace exceeded $40 billion dollars annually.[4]

Business Week estimates the cost to business of stress-related problems and mental illness is $150 billion annually in health insurance, disability claims, lost productivity, and other expenses.[5]

These stress-related facts are enough to give you a headache—which is also quite common. An estimated fifteen tons of aspirin are consumed every day.[6]

The pace and condition of our lives is illustrated by the young mother who called for a taxi cab late one afternoon. When the driver arrived, she brought out three young children and put them in the back seat. "Start the meter, and I'll be back in a few minutes," she directed.

Twenty minutes later the woman returned and asked, "What do I owe you?"

The puzzled driver responded, "Aren't you going any place?"

"No," the woman replied. "I just needed a few quiet moments to myself."[7]

Stressed? Irritable? Fatigued? Procrastinating? Stretched? Bored? Declining sense of humor? Emotionally tapped? Worried? Join the crowd. These consequences are reflected in lives struggling to maintain balance in an imbalanced world. "Reality," said Lily Tomlin, "is the leading cause of stress amongst those still in touch with it."[8]

You've heard all the clichés. Stress is inevitable. If you are alive, you will experience stress. Life events or situations causing stress may be pleasant or unpleasant. You can't hide from it, run away from it, or eliminate it. Stress is the wear and tear of life. Your ability to deal effectively with stress is central to your personal and professional success. And all the world's people said, "Amen. Now what?"

The last thing we need is to rehash what is already common knowledge about stress management. Volumes of stress management material have been written over the last several years, and yet the consequences continue to threaten our lives. We need to do something with all the information and knowledge we possess. Maybe we can provide a bit of practical assistance for fine-tuning our stress management so we can move beyond survival into significant living.

The Concorde was a phenomenal aircraft. Tremendous heat is generated on the exterior of the plane as it flies at supersonic speed. The temperature on the external surface of the plane can reach 127 degrees Centigrade (261 degrees Fahrenheit) even though the outside air temperature is -56 degrees Centigrade (-69 degrees Fahrenheit).

This increased heat causes the plane to expand nine inches longer at cruising speed. The cabin floor of the airplane is uniquely designed on rollers and doesn't expand. A special air conditioning system keeps the inside temperature constant. While the outside of the Concorde experiences tremendous stress, the inside remains comfortable.[9]

The outer person is continually pressed, pushed and pressured from every direction. We are required to expand in order to survive, and our ultimate challenge is to maintain inner courage, calm, and comfort.

The possibility of living healthier lives is within our grasp. It's not the condition of the world that gets us in trouble, but what we tell ourselves about the world. External events, circumstances, and demands can seem overwhelming, but what really matters is our condition inside.

Anthony Robbins, in his book *Awaken the Giant Within*, describes three fundamental actions you need to take to make changes in your life. First, you must believe that a change is needed. Second, you need to believe that you are the person who can change your life. And last, you need to believe that change is possible.[10] Without these three beliefs, you will find it difficult to practice a lifestyle that gives you a sense of control.

I'm using the word *lifestyle* as an acrostic for nine life-enhancing, career-enriching, stress-reducing principles. Check your personal thermometer against these benchmarks.

L isten to what your insides are telling you. Your head, heart, and stomach are built-in stress barometers. Recognizing the presence of stress and being sensitive to your body's warning signals will give you a head start on reducing the damage caused by stress. Avoiding the symptoms or pretending they don't exist is unwise, not to mention unhealthy.

People are often reluctant to admit they are experiencing increased fatigue, excessive anxiety, uncharacteristic moodiness, digestive problems, helplessness, or feelings of depression. The list could go on and on. When your body sends signals that something isn't right, listen. This is your alarm system. It doesn't always mean you're stressed, but it's a pretty good clue.

Insist on a proper perspective. Life's stressors can be overwhelming, and to minimize the intensity of your challenges would be insensitive. However, each of us must recognize the tendency to blow a situation out of proportion by conjuring up in our mind the worst possible scenario.

Earle Wilson defined perspective as, "The ability to see the present moment and immediate event against the background of a larger reference."[11] Keep your imagination in check by focusing on the potential good results and viewing the current circumstances in light of the bigger picture. When life seems to be at its worst, take the time to discover the multitude of blessings you enjoy.

Forego what you can't control. People who frequently complain about feeling burned out are often those who expend considerable energy dealing with things over which they have no control. Their lives are driven by things, people, and events they can't do anything about. Dr. Paul Rosch advised: "Find what things you can have some control over, and come up with creative ways to take control."[12]

Try this. The best way to get in control is to give up control. Sometimes you have no control over a situation and it is a waste of psychological and physical energy to try to change what you cannot change. Accept it.

People who feel in control realize they always have control over how they will interpret or respond to the events. So, instead of giving control to their boss, a crazy driver, the weather, financial challenges, unrealistic expectations, or demanding people, the in-control person determines a response he can control that minimizes a painful result. Dr. Gerald Loren Fishkin said, "You can choose to see yourself as a helpless victim, pointing the finger of blame toward others, but being preoccupied with your role as a 'victim' blinds you to the opportunities that exist in every moment of your life."[13]

End perfectionism. Perfectionism is a great way to increase stress. Where did you ever get the idea that you could be or should be perfect? Who told you everything in life had to go the way you had planned? There is a tremendous push to perform with excellence today. That's a far cry, though, from being perfect. Do your best with what you have. Be realistic about your own performance and the expectations you have of other people. Relax your standards. Have a forgiving spirit for undesirable events and people who disappoint you.

No matter what you think, you are not a superperson able to leap tall buildings with a single bound. Judges might not score you a perfect ten. "Admirable as the idea is," says Dr. George Stevenson in his *How to Deal with Your Tensions,* "it is an open invitation to failure. No one can be perfect in everything. Decide which things you do well, and put your major effort into ... (Don't) take yourself to task if you can't achieve the impossible."[14]

Spiritual well-being precedes being well. This is a marvelous starting point. Some people tend to think their shoulders are broad enough to carry whatever load they encounter. Actually, once you turn everything over to God and allow Him to work through you, incredible strength will surface to help you carry your portion of the load. The Bible says, "Cast all your anxiety on him because he cares for you." [15] It should be a relief to know that you're not expected to deal with pressures, stressors, and disappointments on your own.

Corrie Ten Boom suffered miserably in concentration camps because she helped Jews escape from the Nazis. Her incredible faith allowed her to reflect, "I know that the experiences of our lives, when

we let God use them, become the mysterious and perfect preparation for the work He will give us to do."[16] That's spiritual well-being.

Talk to someone but not just anyone. It should go without being
said that you should avoid negative, worrying, down-in-the-
mouth people who will snuff out what little energy you have left.
Preferably you will choose someone who is accepting, nonjudg-
mental, noncritical, and sincerely interested in your best interests.
Find a respected listener with whom you can talk out your tensions.

Give up the pretense that seeking support is an admission of
weakness. Quite the opposite is true. Only the strong have the
courage to admit they don't have all the answers and are secure
enough to seek out the wisdom of other people.

You are responsible. Jump-start your life by realizing that no one
is coming to your rescue. You are responsible for you. Rarely
will your problems disappear by your pretending they don't exist.
If certain lifestyle patterns and behaviors are causing you difficulty,
take responsibility for making the necessary adjustments. Don't
wait for someone to come along to bail you out. You may wait for a
long time with no satisfactory relief.

A prevailing mystery is why people continually indulge in behav-
ioral, mental, and emotional activities that create unwanted stress
in their lives. Either people believe what they are doing is actually
healthy or they find it easier to wallow in their misery than to do
something about it. If you want release from this vicious cycle, ask
yourself: "What action can I take right now to make this situation
better?" Then do it.

Look outward. An unfortunate consequence occurs when you
become distressed. Your attention turns increasingly inward.
Pondering your predicament and concentrating on yourself
becomes an obsession. The minute you sense this is happening,
reach out to help someone else. Dr. Hans Selye, the respected stress
specialist, puts it this way, "Earn your neighbor's love."[17]

Do one thing for someone every day for which they cannot
repay you. Focus on understanding rather than being understood,

on loving rather than being loved. Count to one thousand before saying or doing anything that could be hurtful to someone else. Go make things right with someone where tension has kept you from enjoying each other's company. Quit keeping score. Say, "I'm sorry, I was wrong." Celebrate others' successes. You'll be absolutely amazed how helping someone else will help to heal yourself.

Enjoy life. This is the ultimate catch-all principle. Enjoying life involves everything from doing absolutely nothing and learning to relax, to taking that vacation you've been putting off. Allow yourself to think positive thoughts, cultivate your sense of humor, and force yourself to have at least one good belly laugh every day. Spend 90 percent of your time generating solutions for the problems you face, and allow yourself to consider creative solutions that, until now, you were afraid to try.

Take a hot bath or cool shower, walk in the rain, run on the beach, breathe deep, enjoy a sunrise, savor a sunset, start a new hobby, revive an old one, treat yourself by buying that special item you've always wanted, sleep in, schedule private time, and probably most important, learn to live one day at a time.

> People burn out, I suspect, not because they have too much to do, but because they get exhausted by the trivial and the inconsequential.
>
> —Rev. Louis Lotz[18]

Chapter 15

LEARN THE LESSONS OF FAILURE

Unfortunately, if you haven't learned the lesson of failure, you'll invariably get the wrong message from your success.

—Harvey Mackay[1]

F AILURE IS PART OF SUCCESS," teaches Ty Boyd. "You must expect to fail again and again and again before you can accomplish anything worthwhile."[2]

Lucy, the famous philosopher from the *Peanuts* cartoon, is counseling and consoling a distraught baseball player after a humiliating loss. "We learn more from losing," she proclaims, "than we do from winning." In the next frame, a frantic Charlie Brown throws up his hands and concedes, "That makes me about the smartest person in the world."[3]

There are days when I feel like Charlie Brown. I've even asked God how smart He wants me to get because if failure increases my intellect, I'll soon be invited to join the National Mensa Society. I know I'm not alone, and even though I've not warmed up to the idea of welcoming failure, I have realized that failure puts me on the fast track to future success.

Orville Redenbacher experimented for years until he successfully developed what my son and a multitude of other people consider to be the best popcorn in the world.[4]

Thousands of literary masterpieces were rejected over and over before being accepted for publication.

Michael Jordan was cut from his high school football team.[5]

It took Paul Ehrlich years of research before discovering formula 606 that could treat those afflicted with syphilis.[6]

Consider the group of ladies who, in 1962, decided to begin a singing career. Their first record was a flop. The second was a failure. The third was a total fiasco, and records four through nine also did not enjoy public appeal.

Determined not to let a few failures stand in their way, they appeared on Dick Clark's *American Bandstand,* hoping that this national exposure would be the ticket to their success. It didn't happen.

Then in the summer of 1964 they cut a record with the lead song entitled "Where Did Our Love Go." The rest, as they say, is history. The Supremes had become know as the "No-Hit Supremes," but they preserved through their failure and disappointments to create their dream career.[7]

Through their repeated failures, the Supremes maintained Winston Churchill's belief that, "Success is going from failure to failure without a loss of enthusiasm."[8] You always pass failure on the way to success. The important test is how we perceive and deal with failure as it threatens our dreams. Edwin Louis Cole offered this insight: "We must be willing to accept responsibility for failure before we are able to accept responsibility for success. God wants to bring us back to each failed test ready to pass it, to replace our failure with success, and to move on."[9] Here are a few thoughts to keep your enthusiasm and your desire alive when you encounter setbacks:

- Failure doesn't mean you'll never achieve your goals. It does mean you will have to try another way.
- Failure doesn't mean you don't have what it takes to succeed. It does indicate additional refinement of your abilities.
- Failure doesn't mean you'll never succeed. It might mean you'll have to learn patience.
- Failure doesn't mean you should give up. It does mean you need to evaluate your commitment, courage, and determination to get back up and press on.
- Failure doesn't mean you should endorse avoiding failure as a motivator. It is an indicator that your risk quotient is being challenged.
- Failure doesn't mean you are inferior. It means you are fallible like the rest of the human race.
- Failure doesn't mean you have wasted your effort. It does mean your effort will need to be redirected.
- Failure doesn't mean you should run and hide. It means should should accept responsibility, admit your failure, learn from it, and get on with the correction.

The question is not whether you will fail. The pertinent question is when will you fail and how will you handle it when it occurs. Everyone experiences flops, fiascoes, fumbles, and failures in life. You already know that. And I know that when you are in the midst of a failure, it isn't comforting to hear that everyone in the world has been there. What matters is that you are there right now.

Reread the eight tips I shared. Don't get too philosophical or mystical about it, but glance back at the failure you experienced and get on with your life. If you keep staring backwards at past events, it's impossible to enjoy the present or future view. Failure fighters learn from the past and let go of it. Failure fretters stare at the past and get stuck in it. Be a fighter.

> I am not judged by the number of times I fail, but by the number of times I succeed; and the number of times I succeed is in direct proportion to the number of times I can fail and keep trying.
>
> —Tom Hopkins[10]

LIVE TO LEARN
AND LEARN
TO LIVE

Chapter 16

No Coasting Allowed

Growing and learning are healthy, normal experiences. Both have to do with a process...and that process is sometimes painful, often slow, and occasionally downright awful! It's like taking three steps forward and two steps back.

—Charles R. Swindoll[1]

FAST FOOD. TEN-MINUTE OIL CHANGE. Instant cash. Direct deposit. Quick photo processing. Express lane check out. One-hour dry cleaning. Today's lifestyles are saturated with instant everything. Life comes at us like a bolt of lightning these days—fast and without warning. But the speed of life contains amazing possibilities for people who are prepared.

Chuck Swindoll's observation that growing and learning is often like taking three steps forward and two steps back, provides an accurate visual image of the difficulty in keeping up. You can't do everything as fast as the world is moving. The quest for success requires you to carefully choose your three steps forward based on what is most necessary for you to keep up. Then, push yourself intently in that direction. One thing is sure, coasting isn't an option.

Instead of dillydallying around, spreading yourself too thin, attempting to be everything to everybody, determine what priorities will get your attention. Carefully examine your job. Which responsibilities produce the greatest results? Begin there, and start identifying ways to continuously improve. You'll achieve more impressive results by becoming 10 percent better in ten areas than 100 percent better in one area or 1 percent better in a hundred areas.

We need to invest continually in personal growth to remain a well-rounded, effective, cutting-edge professional. How many books have you read in the past year? Have you listened to any good educational audiotapes recently? How many professional journals, educational magazines or internet learning services do you consistently peruse? How many seminars or classes have you attended since graduation? Do you have a mentor or life coach to encourage you, challenge you, and provide guidance for your growth? When you commit yourself to a regimen of accelerated growth, your odds for survival, satisfaction, and success improve.

The level of skill that helped you get where you are will not be sufficient to move you into the future. Even ten, twenty, or thirty years of experience is no guarantee that you'll continue to deliver the goods the world has come to expect. Your rate of growth must equal or exceed the rate of change. Investing in spiritual, financial, social, mental, physical, family, and career development is a prerequisite for releasing your potential and adding value to your organization.

Cullen Hightower suggested, "The human body was designed to walk, run or stop; it wasn't built for coasting."[2] That's good to know, because continual movement and improvement is today's universal modus operandi. Become a little bit better today than you were yesterday. Keep moving. Keep stretching. It puts you one step closer to your potential and prepared for today's swift changes.

> There are two kinds of people: the ones who have to be told and the ones who figure it out all by themselves.
>
> —Tom Clancy[3]

Chapter 17

GET CURIOUS

Only the curious will learn and only the resolute overcome the obstacles to learning. The quest quotient has always excited me more than the intelligence quotient.

—Eugene S. Wilson[1]

C ONTINUOUS LEARNING DOESN'T OCCUR BY chance. You must diligently pursue it. Curiosity is a human quality that affords you valuable opportunities. William A. Ward believed, "Curiosity is the wick in the candle of learning."[2] I guess it could be said then, that without curiosity the learning candle is rendered virtually nonexistent.

To the interested person, life experiences are packaged with innumerable possibilities for expanding knowledge. Your mind must be placed in the learning mode to take advantage of these situations.

Portia Nelson wrote a poem entitled, "Autobiography in Five Short Chapters." It reads:

Chapter One
I walk down the street.
>There is a deep hole in the sidewalk.
>I fall in.
>I am lost...I am helpless.
>>It isn't my fault.
It takes forever to find a way out.

Chapter Two
I walk down the same street.
>There is a deep hole in the sidewalk.
>I pretend I don't see it.
>I fall in again.
I can't believe I am in the same place.
>But, it isn't my fault.
It still takes a long time to get out.

Chapter Three
I walk down the same street.
>There is a deep hole in the sidewalk.
>I *see* it is there.
>I still fall in...It's a habit...
>>my eyes are open.
>>I know where I am.
It is *my* fault.
I get out immediately.

Chapter Four
I walk down the same street.
>There is a deep hole in the sidewalk.
>I walk around it.

Chapter Five
I walk down another street.[3]

Poet Archibald MacLeish once said, "There is only one thing more painful than learning from experience, and that is not learning from experience."[4]

How many experiences do you repeat every day without ever asking, "Why am I doing this?" Think of all the people you live with, socialize with, or work with that you've not learned anything new from because you've not been curious enough to get to know them better. What habitual ways of doing things restrict you from escaping your learning comfort zone? What holes do you repeatedly fall in because you've not considered taking another street?

If you want to expand the dimensions of your life, there must be an insatiable desire to not only expand your experiences but also to allow your suppressed curiosity to find out more.

Traveling as a professional speaker provides ample opportunities for me to expand my curiosity. As the ever profound Yogi Berra once said, "You can observe a lot just by watching."[5] Watching has become one of my favorite forms of entertainment and the source of interesting learning. Some of the things I'm curious about aren't necessarily significant, but they do keep my mind churning, thinking, and exploring.

For instance, why don't airplane manufacturers build airplanes from the same material they build the infamous "black box?" Why is the back seat in 80 percent of our nation's taxis as hard as a rock? Why do cars have spare tires but no spare batteries or even a spare fan belt? Why can't the temperature in hotel conference rooms be conducive to human survival? Who comes up with the crazy sayings on airline barf bags?

As a father of two children, I asked a question repeatedly during the Christmas season: "Why don't toy manufacturers include batteries with their toys?" Another favorite: "Who decided 80 percent of children's toys should come unassembled?"

Driving down the highways in rural Iowa can be even more enlightening. I grew up working on my grandfather's farm, but I never questioned a multitude of daily encounters with farm life.

For instance, why do cows chew their cud? For that matter, what is a cud? And, why do they spend so much time chewing it? Well, I got curious.

Cows first fill their stomachs with grass and other food. Then they settle down for a good, long, enjoyable chew. They bring the food back up from their stomachs and rework what they've already eaten, reexperiencing its goodness and transforming it into rich milk.

Chewing the cud—a process of meditating on turning alfalfa into bodybuilding milk. Maybe it's not the most exciting thing you've learned this week, but it's fun and life-enriching to enlarge your understanding of life's most simple experiences.

A few additional topics have piqued my curiosity recently. Why do they lock the bathrooms in gas stations? I don't think anyone is going to break in and clean them. Why do we announce power outages on television or on the city's Web site? Is there another word for synonym? Why is the word *abbreviation* so long?

You'd be amazed how such curious thinking will allow you to expand your horizons.

> In the end, it is important to remember that we cannot become what we need to be by remaining what we are.
>
> —Max DePree[6]

Chapter 18
HOW INFORMED ARE YOU?

What's an expert? I read somewhere that the more a man knows, the more he knows, he doesn't know. So I suppose one definition of an expert would be someone who doesn't admit out loud that he knows enough about a subject to know he doesn't really know much.

—Malcolm S. Forbes[1]

PERHAPS YOU HAVE READ ABOUT the work of Professor Herb Dordick while at the University of Southern California Annenberg School of Communications. Professor Dordick divides people into two categories: First are those who are "being informed" and the other group are those who are "getting informed."

The 10 percent of the population who are "getting informed" actively pursue new information. According to Professor Dordick, "Those 'being informed' are the ones inundated with information who have no strategy to separate the noise and clutter from that which is useful, valuable, and which fuels their innovation machine."[2]

Bill McGowan, the founder of MCI Telecommunications Corporation, believed in getting informed. He read four hours a day and considered it a necessity for staying abreast of today's changing world. According to a feature story in *Success Magazine,* McGowan ran across an idea-producing article in a 1982 issue of the *Stanford Business School Magazine* entitled, "The Skunkworks." It told about a group of Lockheed entrepreneurs who developed, in record time, the U-2 spy plane separately from Lockheed's regular design bureaucracy. As McGowan read, he became excited, for the article explained and reinforced theories he'd been thinking about. Maybe the same concept would work on a unique project he had in mind. As a result, he established a "skunkworks" task force down the block and away from headquarters. The result, only nine months later, was MCI Mail, the company's electronic mail service.[3]

Getting informed and keeping informed produces knowledge that, when applied, generates substantial payoffs. Knowledge is the link between problems and solutions. It provides a bridge to cross from possibilities to inventions, from ideas to discoveries, and from action to results.

When Henry Ford experienced a breakdown in his electrical generators in Dearborn, Michigan, he knew the resulting stalled production line would produce disastrous results. Local electricians were unable to solve his problem, so Mr. Ford contacted his friend Charlie. Charlie Steinmetz was a well-informed electrical engineer. He knew his stuff.

Steinmetz walked into the plant and surveyed the problem. He tinkered here and tinkered there. Ford's employees questioned his supposed electronic genius. In fact, they went to Henry Ford and exclaimed, "This guy doesn't know what he's doing. He just walks the plant and tinkers around." Ford assured them that Charlie knew what he was doing.

Charlie entered the plant the next morning to continue his tinkering. He walked over to the generators, flipped the switch, and machines began humming. Within a few minutes, everything was back to normal. The Ford employees stood in disbelief with their mouths hanging open.

Steinmetz sent Henry Ford a bill for $10,000. Ford responded, "Charlie, you're a great friend but isn't $10,000 a bit much for some tinkering around?"

Charlie immediately replied, "I'm only charging you $10 for tinkering around and $9,990 for *knowing where* to tinker."[4]

We're all like Charlie Steinmetz. Our value is based on what we know and our ability to put what we know to use. Getting informed, being knowledgeable, and increasing our desire and ability to learn are of paramount importance in this vastly changing world. Without this lifestyle, we become a mere expense, a liability.

Robert Heller suggested in the *Super Manager* that you "Get to know what it is you don't know as fast as you can."[5] If you want to avoid falling victim to changing conditions, equip yourself with more than a smattering of semi-useful information. Find out what you need to learn and unlearn to ensure your survival.

Do you have the knowledge necessary to make informed decisions? Are you continually scrambling to understand the specific information required to take appropriate action and produce desired results? Do you have a passion to be the expert in your field? Are you taking advantage of situations that will advance your understanding and expertise? These are the collective abilities of people capable of remaining on the cutting edge.

The philosopher Goethe reflected, "All the knowledge I possess everyone else can acquire, but my heart is exclusively my own."[6] Information without the ambition to apply it is like a bird without wings. It is only a nicety incapable of producing what is necessary.

"Knowledge is only potential power," wrote Napoleon Hill. "It becomes power only when, and if, it is organized into definite plans of action and directed to a definite end."[7] Realize that the difference between people who grow and live life enthusiastically and people who stagnate is often their commitment to apply what they know.

This discussion isn't intended to suggest that you must know everything there is to know about everything. Theodore Roosevelt told the delightful story of a business person who had consulted an attorney for legal advice. Having coffee with a friend one day, he recounted the experience.

"Why did you spend your hard-earned money for a lawyer?" asked the friend. "The law books in his office contain every answer you could ever want. Why didn't you just read the right book and find out the answer for yourself? It would have saved you a lot of money."

"That's true," replied the business person, "but the difference is the lawyer knew what book and what page the answer was on."[8]

I'm glad I can depend on other people's knowledge to assist me in some areas of my life. I can't repair a kitchen faucet, fix the brakes on my car, or do my own income tax. But I do hire people who know what they are doing and are considered the experts in their chosen field. There's simply too much knowledge out there for me to learn in a lifetime. That's why it's so important for me to stay focused on the information I can apply in my specific arena. In this way, others can depend on me in my area of expertise.

We must dedicate ourselves to becoming lifelong learners. We must continually seek out resources and people willing to share their knowledge. There is no final graduation day for those who want to grow and prosper.

"That's all fine and dandy," you say, "but I don't have time for reading, listening, and attending seminars." Neither did John Wesley. But his passion for reading was so intense he made it a part of his schedule. He read mostly on horseback. Wesley rode between fifty and ninety miles a day with a book propped up in his saddle...and got through thousands of volumes during his lifetime.[9] Any more excuses? Become a sponge. Absorb and soak up everything you can.

"The older I get," said Abraham Lincoln, "the more I realize that there is but one wealth, one security on this earth, and this is found in the ability of a person to perform a task well. And first and foremost, this ability must start with knowledge."[10] Get informed!

> The expression for learning in Chinese is made up of two symbols: One stands for studying, the other for practicing constantly. So, you cannot think of learning without thinking of practicing constantly.
>
> —Peter Senge[11]

Chapter 19

IGNITE YOUR INNOVATIVE SPIRIT

Nothing limits achievement like small thinking; nothing expands possibilities like unleashed imagination.

—William Arthur Ward[1]

JEROME LEMELSON IS RESPONSIBLE FOR such gizmos as fax machines, VCRs, cordless phones, and cassette players. The premier inventor is the fourth largest patent-holder in United States history and contributes his innovative success to continually finding problems to solve. He also asks questions regularly. His favorites are, "Is this the best way to do it? Is there a better way?"[2]

Before Dick Fosbury appeared on the high-jump scene, the conventional way for high jumpers to cross the bar had been with a forward leap.

Fosbury introduced the world to a far different technique at the 1968 Olympics in Mexico City. He took four or five bounding strides and lifted himself off the ground. Then, in midair, he did something no Olympic athlete had ever done. He turned his back to the bar, and cleared it. With an Olympic record leap of seven feet, four and one-quarter inches, his new "Fosbury Flop" became the standard. He found a better way by not imitating what others had done before.[3]

Discontinue accepting everything as it is. We need to rethink and possibly reinvent everything we do. It is a matter of survival in our fast-paced, changing world. Question the rules, traditions, and conformity that block innovation. Begin asking, "What do we currently do that we could stop doing?" "What do we have that we don't need?" "What aren't we doing that we should start doing?" "What do we need that we don't have?"

"That all sounds fine," you say, "but I haven't been trained enough to pull this off." Some of the most successful entrepreneurs in our country knew nothing about the business they started. A host of famous artists couldn't draw. There are musicians who can't read music.

Remember the Beatles? They produced over one hundred seventy songs and took the global music scene by storm. At one time, their records accounted for a whopping 60 percent of all U.S. music sales. Here's the irony. John Lennon and Paul McCartney couldn't read or write music. Amazing. Don't think you can't create something of value just because you don't have the education or training to do it. In fact, you probably have a head start.

Learn to foster new ideas by placing yourself in learning situations. Genius blooms in originality. Experts tend to think in structured ways and thereby inhibit their ingenuity. Innovative thinking begins with forgetting or deliberately placing conventional thinking on the back burner. Unlearning what you've learned allows your mind to flow freely.

Look at things through fresh eyes. Think like a beginner with no preconceived idea of how things should work, what things fit where, and how simple life tasks should be completed.

You'll be amazed at what an innovative expert you can become by acting like a beginner. You might also discover some wonderful things about yourself, your potential, and the world around you.

The guy who invented the first wheel was an idiot. The guy who invented the other three, he was a genius.

—Sid Caesar[4]

Section Six

RETHINK WHAT YOU THINK

Chapter 20

ACCENTUATE THE POSITIVE

Keep your face always toward the sunshine—and shadows will
fall behind you.

—Walt Whitman[1]

A SMALL PLANT GROWS IN THE Australian bush country. Called the "sundew," it has a slender stem and tiny round leaves fringed with hairs that glisten with bright drops of fluid. Attractive and harmless red, white, and pink blossoms adorn the plant. But look out for the leaves. They are deadly. The shiny moisture on each leaf is sticky and will imprison any bug or insect that flirts with it. As the insect struggles to get free, the vibration triggers the leaves to close tightly around it.[2] The innocent-looking plant then feeds on its victim.

The leaves of negativity: moaning, groaning, complaining, and self-pity appear harmless. But the deadly traps suffocate your ability to maintain an objective view of your experiences. They put you on the fast track to discouragement and depression.

Have you ever known anyone who seems to be against every-thing? Just listen to the conversations around you. Churches, communities, committees, organizations, and even families are being inundated with what's wrong. No matter how positive something is, someone is there to see the dark side. Their life consists of taking the contrary view to most every issue. A mindset is created wherein they believe it is their obligation to point out life's negatives to the world. What a miserable and restrictive lifestyle. And what good does it do? Zippo. Zero. Absolutely nothing constructive.

Helen Keller's comment deserves our attention. If our minds are constantly focused on what's wrong, we'll block any sunshine in our shadow prone world. This form of pessimistic mania is psychologically fatal and infectious. The amount of energy expended in this lifestyle is phenomenal. Accentuating the positive might require a thought transfusion and a heavy regimen of optimism to overcome current self-imposed misery, but it will be well worth whatever effort it takes.

Dan Millman, writing in *Way of the Peaceful Warrior*, said: "Your mind is your predicament. It wants to be free of change, free of pain, free of obligations of life and death. But change is a law, and no amount of pretending will alter that reality."[3] You have the ability to alter the impact of change. What you think about, say about, and do about change will determine your attitude toward it and your ability to deal with it. You see in every situation what you have conditioned yourself to see. The way you mentally interpret what's happening is far more important than the event itself.

Accentuate the positive by:

- Remembering your choices
- Staying focused on purpose
- Maintaining a sense of humor
- Looking beyond the present situation,
- Accepting negative emotions, dealing with them, and moving on
- Eliminating negativity

- Behaving in a manner consistent with the way you want to feel
- Creating fun in your daily experiences

Peak performers maintain a positive and productive attitude toward change. Here is the simple reason: By concentrating on what's going right, you boost your ability to deal with change. Accentuating the positive is a habit worth pursuing. Now, don't think this transformation can happen overnight. Be patient with yourself and those around you, but maintain an earnest commitment to begin using your energies to create new ideas, pursue dreams, and capitalize on the benefits that change produces. You'll be amazed at how energized you become.

> Life has, indeed, many ills, but the mind that views every object in its most cheering aspect, and every doubtful dispensation as replete with latent good, bears within itself a powerful and perpetual antidote.
>
> —Lydia H. Sigourney[4]

Chapter 21

BREAK THE CHAINS

Impossible is a word to be found only in the dictionary of fools.
—Napoleon Bonaparte[1]

R AMANANDA, A WIRY 107-POUND MAN from India, sat in the middle of a University of Minnesota auditorium floor on a warm August evening. Dr. O. P. Tiwari of Chicago described him to the audience. "Please don't forget Ramananda is sixty-eight. He's a medical miracle who's done five thousand push-ups non-stop."

A chain with links of half-inch steel was brought out. "Come and try to pull it apart," Dr. Tiwari challenged the audience. Ten people, five on each end, had no effect at all.

The six-foot chain was wrapped around Ramananda's waist, strung between his bended legs, and connected to a metal bar under his feet. "You will now see what can happen if the mind is under control," Dr. Tiwari announced.

The spindly little man, sitting on the floor, braced himself against the bar under his feet. His body tensed; then the legs plunged forward. The chain broke in the middle of a link![2]

My first reaction was, "That's impossible!" And, for me, it probably is, not because of the chains around the body but because of the chains I place around my expectations. Charles Kettering was addressing this issue when he said, "It's amazing what ordinary people can do if they set out without preconceived notions."[3]

Nothing ordinary or splendid is ever achieved except by those who dare to believe that their inner strength is greater than the challenge. This chain-breaking attitude opens the door to virtually unlimited opportunities.

Swimmer Susie Maroney split the chain of impossibility by completing the one hundred twelve-mile swim between Cuba and the Florida Keys.

Maroney, age twenty-two, made it ashore twenty-four and one-half hours after leaving Havana, becoming the first woman to swim across the Florida Straits. She emerged from the surf sunburned and welted from jellyfish stings, but also with the knowledge she had done what no other woman had ever done. "So many times you think, 'I just don't want to keep going,'" she said, her tongue swollen from the salt water. "My body is aching all over."[4]

Doug Larson once said, "Some of the world's greatest feats were accomplished by people not smart enough to know they were impossible."[5] Maybe some of us aren't as smart as we think we are. What chains are binding you from accomplishment? What doubts and fears tend to creep into your mind whenever you consider a challenging task?

Breaking the chains isn't a matter of climbing a higher mountain, swimming a farther distance, or building a bigger business. It's about conquering yourself—your hopes, your fears.

What could you do if you didn't know what you could do?

> I think it's interesting how much we can accomplish before we find out we can't do something.
>
> —General Leslie Groves[6]

Chapter 22

DON'T POISON THE ENVIRONMENT

The poison of pessimism creates an atmosphere of wholesale
negativism where nothing but the bad side of everything is
emphasized.

—Charles Swindoll[1]

BELLYACHERS, MOANERS, AND GROANERS POISON the world
with their verbal pollution. It's a frustrating problem.
Everybody suffers from it. Many contribute to it. Only a few
realize they are doing it.

Psychology Today ran an article about a man who committed
three hours a day for ten years to complaining. Each day he'd call,
write, or talk to someone about what he thought was wrong with the
world.[2] Rather than changing anything, the article concluded that
the only result of this exercise was that it made the man incredibly
miserable.

Verbal poisoning is highly contagious, especially for people who
work or live together. When you are surrounded by professional
grumblers it's easy to get caught up in the habit. Beware of becoming
one of these environment destroyers.

Catastrophizers. They blow everything out of proportion. Little irritants become giant problems. If one thing is wrong, everything is wrong. If one person in a department is difficult to deal with, a generalization is made that the entire department is bad. One young person with challenging behaviors is soon viewed as the entire youth population. Look out for the person with refined embellishing skills. See things as they really are, not through a misguided, tainted magnifying glass.

Whiners. These people look like they were weaned on dill pickles. They wake up negative and proceed through the day making their list of why life is unfair. Sob stories, a "poor me" attitude, and a feeling of helplessness make up their daily agenda.

They sponsor frequent "pity parties" so others know they are undervalued and unappreciated. Whiners are the leaders in living unhappy, unfulfilled lives. Their belief that the world is out to get them and to give them a lifetime of trouble results in a prison of discontent, built with their own hands.

Bad Finders. Just as it sounds, the bad finder has decided his life's job description is to find everything bad in the world to him and to the people around him. Interestingly enough, bad finders possess an external perfectionist attitude. Why external? They believe everything and everyone outside of themselves should be perfect, but there is always something wrong. They believe they have little or no control in their lives, other people cause the problems, and change creates insurmountable problems.

This personality is characterized by the following story of a mother taking her son to school. As they pulled up in front of the school, the little boy says, "Mommy, we didn't see any idiots today." "No, son we didn't," Mom replied. "Why did you say that?" "Yesterday, when Daddy took me to work, we saw seven idiots on the way."

Cynics. Have you ever known anyone who is against everything? The greatest miracle in the world could occur right before their eyes, and their cynical perspective would immediately take over to find a minuscule flaw. Cynics hold themselves as intellectually superior, therefore their job is to keep the rest of us informed of what's wrong with the world. Robert Kennedy once said, "One-fifth of the people are against everything all the time."[3] Those are the cynics. Communities, churches, organizations, and even families plagued with a cynic in their midst live with a continual burden.

Contrary to popular opinion, talk is not cheap. Talk is extremely expensive. What we say powerfully affects us and those around us. Make a pact with yourself to refrain from any conversation that would pollute or poison yourself or those with whom you live, work, or socialize.

> The thing that separates good players from great ones is mental attitude. It might only make a difference of two or three points in an entire match, but how you play those key points often makes the difference between winning and losing. If the mind is strong you can do almost anything you want.
>
> —Chris Evert[4]

Chapter 23

LOOK FOR THE BLUE SKY

The pessimist complains about the wind; the optimist expects it to change; the realist adjusts the sails.

—William Arthur Ward[1]

MARTIN SELIGMAN, IN HIS BOOK *Learned Optimism*, has developed the scientific basis for optimism. According to Seligman, you can either be pessimistic, discouraged, and helpless, or you can be optimistic, positive, courageous, and seek solutions. The choice is up to you. Nobody else is in charge of your attitude. Either way, you are responsible; and you enjoy—or pay—the consequences.[2]

The Oscar-winning movie *Forrest Gump*, a top-ten, all-time money-maker in Hollywood history, was an encouraging display of attitude as a choice. Even though many critics called the movie "simplistic" or "sappy" or just a feel-good movie, I tend to think it offered much more. Maybe those who berated it in critiques were just negative, pessimistic people who felt the message hit too close to home.

Forrest Gump experiences a series of almost unimaginable, unbearable tragedies. He was born with limited intelligence and further plagued with the need to wear braces on his legs. He was constantly teased and tormented by his peers.

Eventually Forrest went to war and had to face the devastating experiences of having his best friend die in his arms and watching his courageous commanding officer lose both legs on the battlefield.

The mother he adored died before his eyes, and the woman he loved since childhood rejected him over and over again. After twenty years of diligent pursuit, Forrest won her over, only to have her die within a few months after their marriage.

The story line didn't reflect a feel-good theme. If Forrest had been brainwashed with today's culture he would have been expected to declare himself a victim and wallow in self-pity. Instead of whining Forrest held fast to his endearing and unshakable optimism, and he frequently voiced his gratitude for what he had. To him "life is like a box of chocolates; you never know what you're gonna get."[3] But the inspiring message here is that no matter what you get, life is only as sweet or sour as you make it. Thank you, Mr. Gump.

You have a choice about what you believe, what your expectations are, and how you respond to life. Your choice is an accurate indicator of the person you really are. People and the world around you ultimately reflect back what you send out.

"A pessimist is one who makes difficulties out of his opportunities," said Harry Truman. "And an optimist is one who makes opportunities out of his difficulties."[4] Optimism isn't some starry-eyed state of mind that believes the future will automatically be ideal. Instead, an optimist learns to act in a way that will create a positive future.

Evidence is building that this positive expectancy helps the optimist withstand discomfort, overcome discouragement, and turn stress into results-oriented energy and drive. Positive expectancy has also been identified with healthy self-confidence and the pursuit of dreams.

Pessimists, on the other hand, feel bad even when they feel good, for fear of how bad they will feel when they feel better. Regardless of how good things are, the pessimist is always bleak about the future. The epitaph on a pessimist's tombstone should read, "I told you this would happen." Of course, "The nice part about being a pessimist," writes George Will, "is that you are constantly being either proven right or pleasantly surprised."[5]

It's amazing how cartoons can drive home a point with only a few words. Such is the case from a classic *Pogo* cartoon from the 1970s. The cartoon was two frames. The setting in frame one showed Pogo standing in a mud hole, looking down at the huge mess surrounding him. The second frame showed Pogo in the same situation but looking up at a beautiful blue sky filled with birds, a few fleecy white clouds, and a bright sun. The captions were simple:

> Frame 1: "You can spend your whole life looking down at the yuck and muck and mire all around your feet, or
>
> Frame 2: You can look up AND SEE THE SKY!"[6]

I recently flew from Florida back to the midwest. Weather reports indicated the midwest was socked in with bad weather. However, the two and one half hours I spent flying at thirty thousand feet were breathtakingly beautiful. The sky was a crisp clear blue, and the sun shone with a glistening brightness. Then we started our descent into the clouds, and the plane began to shake. The sun disappeared, and we were engulfed in the darkness of thick gray clouds. Landing was a little tricky as the forty- to fifty-mile-an-hour wind gusts made a soft landing virtually impossible. As I exited the airport, the cold rain pelted my face, and I thought how ironic it was that only a few minutes earlier I had been enjoying the awesome view above the clouds.

Just as the *Pogo* cartoon illustrated, I realized the sky is always blue. It's just a matter of where you are looking and what you are expecting to see. If in your darkest moments the sky remains clear blue, what are you looking for?

Look for the blue sky!

> An optimist may see a light where there is none, but why must the pessimist always run to blow it out?
>
> —Rene Descartes[7]

Section Seven

STAY BALANCED

Chapter 24

Keep Life's Irritations in Perspective

Man's last freedom is his freedom to choose how he will react in any given situation.

—Victor Frankl[1]

THERE WAS NO REASON TO believe the two-hour and fifty-minute flight from Newark, New Jersey to Minneapolis, Minnesota would involve anything out of the ordinary. However, a cute little blond haired, blue-eyed, two-year-old had a different plan.

The flight was sold out, and it took considerable time for me to reach my seat in the middle of the plane. As I stuffed my briefcase into the overhead compartment, a restless young flyer, unhappy at being strapped in his seat, introduced himself to his plane full of flying companions by squealing, *"Me out!" "Me out!"*

I found my seat and politely introduced myself to the gentleman next to me. It was immediately apparent that he was a nervous flyer and would prefer that the flight was over before it started.

No sooner had I strapped myself in when I heard the little guy across the aisle in the window seat repeat his familiar phrase, *"Me out!"* Then he added a second verse, *"Eee! Eee!"* It was a shrilling and irritating sound.

By the time our 727 jet folded its landing gear and ascended into the heavens I had endured dozens of *"Me out! Eee! Eee!"* combinations. Surely his mother would soon quiet her child and I could comfortably settle in for the remainder of the flight.

But such was not the case. In fact, this little guy possessed a well-developed voice box that allowed him to reverberate his verbal combinations up to ten times a minute. I counted. He possessed unbelievable perseverance.

People within listening distance were becoming visibly irritated. In fact, the young man sitting next to me plugged his ears with his fingers, then buried his head in his hands, and finally excused himself for an extended visit to the rear of the plane. Other travelers put pillows against their ears, and several resorted to airline or personal headphones. No matter how desperately people tried, there was no escaping the audial barrage.

"Me out! Eee! Eee! Eee!" This youngster was intent on "entertaining" us the entire flight. There were a few short-lived pauses to wet his vocal chords with apple juice. Even the airline attendants displayed their agitation by frequently visiting our area and asking the mother if there was anything they could do. She gracefully declined, holding her forefinger in front of her mouth and reminding the little boy to *Shhh!* Every intervention was followed by a brief mischievous smile and then, *"Me out! Me out! Eee! Eee! Eee! Me out!"*

The unknown airline captain was a popular man as he taxied the plane to the gate and moved us all closer to freedom. As the seat belt sign went off several annoyed passengers got to their feet and immediately turned to cast a disgusted glare at their young traveling companion. I must admit, I shot a quick disapproving glance of my own, but quickly smiled, realizing what this boy had achieved.

The little guy remained unfazed. He drew a deep breath and responded to his silent but obvious critics with a final "EEE!" "EEE!" "Me Out!"

As I walked through the airport to catch my connecting flight, I marveled to myself how easily the quality of our airplane ride was tainted by one child's behavior. I was further reminded how every person's reaction was determined, not by the child's behavior, but by our reaction to it.

The events of this flight are not unlike our life encounters. No one can control the action of others or the many events of life which tend to upset us, but we can control our reactions to these behaviors and circumstances.

Your mind and thoughts are your own. You are the controller of every reaction you experience. Only you can decide the impact of your experiences. The simple truth is that you choose your perspective on life.

> There is a technique, a knack, for thinking, just as there is for doing other things. You are not wholly at the mercy of your thoughts, any more than they are you. They are a machine you can learn to operate.
>
> Alfred North Whitehead[2]

Chapter 25

IT'S TIME TO DEAL
WITH OVERLOAD

Next week there can't be any crisis. My schedule is already full.
Henry A. Kissinger[1]

L OOK AROUND AT THE NUMBER of people who are extremely busy but attaining few results. Work has become an accumulation of exhausting activity and effort. Their lives are complicated by too many commitments and not enough energy to give to them all.

Meeting mania. Memo madness. Overwhelming to-do lists. Rushing here and running there. Personal appointments. Family commitments. Confusion over responsibilities. Ringing phones and non-stop messages. Demanding people. Unexpected crises. The list goes on and on.

A Time/CNN poll finds that more than 66 percent of us would like to "slow down and live a more relaxed life," in contrast to only 19 percent who say they would like to "live a more exciting, faster-paced life."[2]

We've become infected with activity overload. This contagious phenomenon happens when our lives are filled to the point of being incapable of handling anything else. Without appropriate action, we are on a one-way street to personal ineffectiveness. An emotional or physical "crash" is waiting just around the corner.

When the trauma of overload occurs with computers, extra disks and quick off-loading are required to make the machine serviceable again. Seldom used information is stored away, big projects receive their own disks, and old stuff is discarded. The "disk full" indicator goes off until such time as overload reoccurs. The computer breathes a sigh of relief and is off and running normally again.

Maybe it's time to evaluate your activity files. Are your energies and talents being activated in directions that leave you feeling fulfilled and satisfied with the results you achieve? Or are you in a reactive mode and hear yourself frequently lamenting:

"There just isn't enough time."
"I have too much to do and so little time to do it."
"I'm so busy."
"I can't handle any more."

There remains an enigma that seems to ignite these complicating attitudes, actions, and lifestyles. It's the mystery of balance. Maintaining equilibrium. Juggling demands. Having a handle on what drives you. Knowing your personal limitations. Living an enabled and empowered life.

The circus tightrope walker stands on a rope high above an anxious crowd. She holds a long bar in her hands and anticipates the balance needed to make the journey to the other side. Adding to the suspense, she climbs on the seat of a unicycle she will pedal across the rope.

The professional tightrope artist knows not to begin until everything is properly aligned. Only then does she begin the slow and careful journey.

If at any time her balance waivers, she must stop to regain her composure. For the tightrope expert, balance is everything. Without it, failure and possible serious injury are certain.

Like the tightrope walker, you need balance in your life to ensure a successful journey. When the pressures cause you to lose your balance, it is important to regain composure before continuing.

There are no shortcuts in the quest for balance. The right tools are important but not enough. Getting from one end of the platform to the other is achieved by walking a straight line determined by the final destination you've chosen. And in the midst of your busyness, stop to ask, "Am I really doing what matters most in my life?"

Reactive people will blame the environment, other people, an overwhelming workload, and a million other factors outside of themselves. Responsive, proactive people determine to take personal responsibility for the quality of their day and the extent of their productivity.

Life is not meant to be lived at breakneck speed. Such a reckless pace leads to overload and exhaustion. Yet past experiences, the expectations of others, and our own attitudes about what we should accomplish have a tremendous influence on us.

What do you presently believe about the "musts" in your daily schedule? Are they really "have-to's?" Do they exist because you've filled your life with "shoulds" and now the only thing left to do is to save face? Often, our lives reflect the interjected demands from outside sources.

Self-imposed expectations like being perfect, remaining strong, pleasing everyone, and a cadre of other possibilities need to be put in perspective. Dismantle the belief that you can't get organized or that there just isn't enough time. Stop finding excuses when deadlines are missed. Quit blaming others or comparing what you are capable of achieving to the accomplishments of others. Take responsibility and do what your ability allows you to do. No less. No more. Enough.

Erase the thought that recklessly running to and fro is a noble lifestyle. Align your activities with the primary purpose in your life. Place that purpose at the top of your "to-do" list each day and remain determined to break away from doing just to do. Your power light will come back on, and you'll be energized to get involved in activities that make a difference.

> No one can maintain more than three priorities. If you have a job you care about, that's a priority. If you have a family, that's a priority. Which leaves one more. Maybe it's staying in shape, maybe it's volunteering at your church. Most people understand this intuitively. But they keep overcommitting themselves and overcomplicating their lives. So my advice is simple: figure out what priorities are, and say no to everything else.
>
> Elaine St. James[3]

Chapter 26

Energize Your Abilities
and Keep Learning

Your ability needs responsibility to expose its possibilities. Do what you can with what you have where you are.

Theodore Roosevelt[1]

Peeople feel busier than ever, but productivity often sags. This paradox of change becomes a vicious circle of busyness without results, leading to greater stress. It, in turn, creates a hesitancy to step out, try new things and people become tentative about using their talents and abilities. The trick to making change work for you is assessing your abilities, focusing on what you do best, activating your self-initiative, and pursuing results.

You've been given a gift of talents and gifts that you've never unwrapped. They are yours, but the ghastly "comfort zone" or fear of the unknown have kept you from stepping out to discover them. Now it is time for you to reevaluate and open yourself up to new possibilities.

Musician Ken Medema was born blind, but his parents made an early decision to treat him as a normal child. Ken grew up learning to play games, ride a bike, water ski, and a host of other "normal" activities.

Ken's parents never denied his condition. They simply affirmed his worth as a human being by focusing on what he could do. Ken developed into a dynamic person with a strong inner wholeness that causes him and those around him to almost forget about his disability.

One day on campus, Ken accidentally bumped into another blind student who said, "Hey, watch it. Don't you know I'm blind?" Instead of drawing attention to his own handicap, Ken apologized. "I'm sorry. I didn't see you."[2]

You and I are frequently bumping into situations that tend to reveal our weaknesses. The reactive approach is to use our weaknesses as excuses. Rather, acknowledge your mistakes, weaknesses, and shortcomings and then **MOVE ON.**

Discomfort is normal. Just don't allow it to be an excuse for inactivity. Don't dwell on what might have been. Refrain from focusing on the negative possibilities. Focus on what you do best. Build on and sharpen your skills. Broaden the demands you place on yourself and you'll be surprised how the resources will surface to help you perform at a new level. Abilities are often hidden treasures waiting to be discovered and energized.

Surviving and thriving today might also require a certain degree of unlearning. In pursuit of an innovative, proactive lifestyle, its best to forget, ignore, and sometimes disobey the old rules, assumptions, and restrictive thoughts that have crammed our brain cells. This formidable challenge will require censoring old beliefs we've held near and dear. It is time to snuff out that which snuffs out your potential to capitalize on camouflaged opportunity. You'll be surprised how much can be discarded, eliminated, and forgotten.

Eric Hoffer said, "In a time of drastic change, it is the learners who inherit the future. The learned find themselves equipped to live in a world that no longer exists."[3] It's no longer acceptable to be satisfied with the current level of knowledge. Build momentum by learning something new, moving forward, stretching yourself, and remaining on the cutting edge of today's demands. With your new knowledge in hand, catch a vision of what could be and relentlessly pursue it.

Numerous studies have been conducted to determine what makes a person creative. Who are those people who explore the unknown to make life meaningful? Those who create their future are optimistic. They are curious, observant, and turn innovative ideas into practical solutions.

Change-masters are open to alternatives while retaining their independent thinking. They expose themselves to new ideas and information, take the time for creatively considering application, and determine how to best turn them into assets. Their openness to new experiences allows them to take risks and not allow naysayers to hold them back. A full commitment to what they are doing makes them action- oriented people who follow their purpose and dreams.

"It is no use saying 'we are doing our best,'" Winston Churchill believed. "You have got to succeed in doing what is necessary."[4] People who are successful today are people who believe they have much to learn but are also confident they have much to share. They may not know exactly what the future holds for them, but they contribute to the best of their ability.

Don't focus on eliminating your weaknesses; you'll spin your wheels. Understand your abilities and put yourself in a position where they can be used. Keep learning what is needed to succeed. Combine with a responsible use of talent, and you'll navigate your way successfully through challenging situations.

> If you want to win anything—a race, your self, your life—you have to go a little berserk.
>
> George Sheehan[5]

Chapter 27

ENJOY THE RIDE

Life, we learn too late, is in the living, in the tissue of every day and hour.

Stephen Leacock[1]

I CHUCKLE EVERY TIME I SEE the advertisements generated from Nissan's newest marketing approach. Implemented in the Fall of 1996, this extremely successful campaign, interestingly enough, doesn't offer a hard sell on Nissan vehicles but rather a light-hearted, catchy script with an attention getting byline. *Life is a journey. Enjoy the ride.*[2]

Life certainly is a journey filled with smooth sailing interstates and bumpy, hard to navigate back roads. There are mountains to conquer and valleys to endure. The odds of experiencing a flat tire, dead battery, over-heated engine, or empty gas tank are pretty good. Most journeys include a few detours, misdirected turns, and even an accident or two along the way.

I would be the first to admit that I often get so caught up in reaching a destination, I fail to enjoy the scenery along the way. I don't appreciate drivers taking their leisurely time, road construction requiring me to negotiate previously untraveled roads, unreasonable speed limits, or stop lights that always turn red when I approach.

The symbolism here is easily transferred to life. As Steven Wright said, "I think God's going to come down and pull civilization over for speeding."[3] Living in a state of constantly driving faster and faster toward a destination without an appreciation for the journey is costly. I've missed great opportunities. My worst attitudes surface. Performance becomes negatively affected. My resistance to, and patience with undesirable events is curbed. In general, my ability to play the hand I've been dealt is severely disabled.

Several years ago a newspaper published a story from the life of Lyndon B. Johnson, former President of the United States. "In Stonewall, Texas, at a ceremony recognizing highway beautification, the President told his audience he was feeling fine because he had followed the advice of an old woman who once said, 'When I walks, I walks slowly. When I sits, I sits loosely. And when I feels worry comin' on, I just goes to sleep.'"[4]

"The trouble with the rat race," said Lily Tomlin, "is that even if you win, you're still a rat."[5] In our uptight, anxiety ridden society many of us would do well to heed the advice given to President Johnson. Considering how short life is and the insanity of the rat race at times, it would behoove us to "sits loosely" and enjoy the ride. In the hustle and bustle to achieve our destinations, let's pledge to pull off at a few rest areas and put things back into perspective. "Smell the perfume of flowers," encouraged Helen Keller. "Taste with relish each morsel, as if tomorrow you could never smell or taste again."[6]

Remember: Do what you love. Love what you do. Balance work and play. Don't forget to live.

Pull off to the side of the road a minute. Even though you cannot go back and make a brand new start, you can start from this moment and determine to enjoy the ride to the end.

My advice to you is not to inquire why or whither, but just enjoy your ice cream while it's on your plate.

Thornton Wilder[7]

Section Eight

LIVE LIFE TO THE FULLEST

Chapter 28

LIVE IN THE NOW

The word 'now' plays a big part in my life. I'm not particularly interested in the ten-year plan. I want to know, what am I doing today? Is this a good day? And amazingly, most of them are good days.

Linda Ellerbee[1]

I N THE CARTOON *GARFIELD*, GARFIELD and his owner Jon were pictured in one of their typical cartoon conversations. Jon is in one of his philosophical moods as he questions whether or not he has lived any former lives.

Garfield throws Jon one of his "you've got to be kidding" looks as he seriously doubts the prospect of Jon's reincarnation because, "You're not even living this life."[2]

Jon's not alone. Some people are so preoccupied with "former" lives or the anticipation of "future" lives that they completely overlook this life. They become obsessed with "what could have been" or "what might be" that they are oblivious to "what is."

I'm well aware of how beneficial it can be to learn from the past and build on it. I'm also an avid believer in living within a future vision I choose for my life. In fact, I'm never happier than when I'm pursuing my dreams for a better life. I'm energized knowing exactly the direction I want my life to go. But, I'm living fully in the moment to make those aspirations a reality.

I've experienced first hand what happens to people so imprisoned by their past that today could hardly be characterized as living. When I worked as a jail administrator I encountered lives that were driven by survival. In the normal world people get caught in ruts, but in the penal system, the rut becomes a grave. Ellen Glasgow said, "The only difference between a rut and a grave is their dimensions."[3] The people I worked with had dug themselves a very small hole that suffocated hope from their lives.

Prisoners rarely take advantage of the structured system to put their past behind them and work to improve the quality of their lives. Once they are sentenced by the courts, a severely restricted mindset dominates their life. Freedom is gone. Personal dignity is diminished. The activities of their day are now dictated to them. Personal identity is replaced with jail uniforms. This is not living— it's existing. And, once in the system, few choose to escape their self-made grave even when the sentence is fulfilled.

I also spent several years working with juvenile delinquent youth. The difference between this population and jail inmates is that I always believed there was a ray of hope for these young people. Maybe they were not yet indoctrinated into an irresponsible lifestyle. The goal was always to help them live each day within acceptable guidelines and create an internal desire to keep the hope for a better life alive. This might sound like a reasonable task but you would be amazed how many young people were firmly connected and comfortable with failure. It was a difficult task to help them change the image they possessed of themselves so they could begin believing a better life was possible.

I came away from these professional experiences with these convictions:

1. The earlier in life we connect people to the value of life, the better our chances for helping them live in the "now."
2. Once we fall into the rut of refusing to take responsibility for our lives, there is little hope for improving the quality of our lives.
3. People who live in a literal, mental, or emotional prison rarely accept responsibility for their current condition.
4. Those who want to do what they want to do when they want to do it often end up in places where people tell them what to do, when and how to do it, and whether or not they'll ever get to do what they want to do again.
5. Unless people view themselves as valuable, lovable, and respectable, they will rarely develop a positive view of life.

The only way to live in the "now" is to accept each minute of every day as an unrepeatable precious moment. It is a valuable gift for which we have the responsibility to take ownership. Love your work. Enjoy your play. Laugh often. Cherish the good times. Shed your tears in the sad times. Believe that whatever happens today is preparation for the challenges, opportunities, and possibilities you'll encounter tomorrow.

> You don't have to be intelligent, good-looking, or rich to get what you want out of life. There are lots and lots of situations which you can use as an excuse to win or as an excuse to fail. Choosing to be responsible for your life puts you in control over it.
>
> W. Mitchell[4]

Chapter 29

Loosen Your Grip

When I grip the wheel too tight, I find I lose control.

Steve Rapson[1]

I WAS FORTUNATE ENOUGH AS A high school junior to land a job at an all new automatic car wash. It was a high tech operation featuring rotating soft brushes, rollers that automatically forwarded the vehicle, and a high powered dryer. (If this doesn't sound very high tech, remember the year was 1969.)

Customers loved the end result but many struggled with the automation. "Please make sure all windows are up, drive your car forward until the stop light flashes, put your car in neutral, and let the machine do the rest," were the instructions I gave to every customer.

Everything went as planned until the conveyor began pushing the car forward and a sudden rush of soap and water blinded people's vision. Customers would frequently hit their brakes, frantically honk their horns, and even attempt to steer their cars, often causing the tires to become jammed against the guide rails.

I can't count the number of times I would be forced to turn off the machine, navigate my way through dripping soap and water to the driver and remind them to relax and let the machine do the work. Soon the car would be propelled into the outside world, washed, polished, and dried.

It was amazing how many times people would return the next week and repeat their blunders. Some people adjusted quickly to giving up control of the car but the majority found it difficult to trust a machine. Ironically, the more they tried to control the situation, the more disastrous the outcome.

Although I never had difficulty in a car wash, I've encountered similar emotions during life situations. When I feel confident and in control, things seem to go quite smoothly. However, when my energies are directed at events beyond my control, I get frustrated, panic, and want to apply the brakes or steer my way clear of the struggle.

There are times in all of our lives when we've followed the instructions, prepared ourselves the best we can, and have aligned our thoughts, attitudes and feelings with the demands of the situation. We're in control. But there are other factors, including other people, extenuating circumstances, or unexpected obstacles that thunderously appear. Suddenly we realize the best laid plans aren't good enough. Relax.

Sometimes, all you can do is all you can do. Put the situation in perspective. Focus on those things you have some ability to control and loosen your grip on the steering wheel. You may be surprised how polished you come out the other side.

> I like living. I have sometimes been wildly, despairingly, acutely, miserable, racked with sorrow, but through it all I still know quite certainly that just to be alive is a grand thing.
>
> Agatha Christie[2]

Chapter 30

HOLD TIGHT TO YOUR PURPOSE

Nothing contributes so much to tranquilize the mind as a steady purpose—a point on which the soul may fix its intellectual eye.

Mary Shelley[1]

IT DOESN'T TAKE A FUTURIST, prophet, or fortune teller to predict your future. I can do it for you. Ready? Let's give it a try. All you need to do is answer this question: What is your purpose in life and what plans have you made to attain it?

You wouldn't believe the varied answers I've received to that question. Some people simply want to exist. Others want lots of money and success. Still others get almost mystical about it. Don't make this philosophical. What do you want out of life? What is your supreme aim? What do you have a burning desire to be and achieve? The question that puts it all in perspective for me is this: "What drives you life?"

Napoleon Hill suggested, "In your struggle for success you should keep constantly in mind the necessity of knowing what it is that you want—of knowing precisely what is your definite purpose—and the value of the principle of organized effort in the attainment of that which constitutes your definite purpose."[2]

Mother Teresa was a marvelous example of Napoleon Hill's advice. She didn't necessarily set out for a career helping the poor. In fact, she taught the wealthiest children of Calcutta, India, for twenty years. Living in the wealthy neighborhood overlooking the impoverished slums kept her contained in comfort.

Walking down the streets below one night, she heard a woman crying out for help. As this dying woman fell into Mother Teresa's arms, her life changed forever. Her purpose was discovered.

She rushed the woman to the hospital and was told to sit and wait. Knowing the woman was in dire need of medical assistance, she took her to another hospital where she was also told she would have to wait. Mother Teresa realized the woman was being denied medical attention because of her social status so she took the woman home where she later died in Mother Teresa's arms.

It was then that this woman of extraordinary courage and compassion pledged this would never happen again. She dedicated her life to easing the pain of the suffering and her purpose was that whether suffering people lived or died, they would do so with dignity. Countless numbers of people have been treated with love and respect like never before because of Mother Teresa.[3]

I doubt Mother Teresa ever got up in the morning and said: "What another lousy day in the changing streets of Calcutta." No way. Every minute of every day of her life was driven by a specific purpose.

Purpose gives us a meaningful and fulfilling reason for living. It keeps us attentive to our life's priorities and increases our tolerance for ambiguity. A compelling purpose provides the motivation for us to do the things we don't like to do, but need to do in order to move us closer to our purpose. Flexibility increases as a renewed positive anticipation of the future emerges. That's the power of purposeful living.

Purpose allows you to keep change in perspective. Those who possess a strong sense of purpose and commitment, who consistently view change as a challenge to master instead of a threat, aren't overwhelmed by the stress of change.

James Allen probably said it best: "They who have no central purpose in life fall easy prey to petty worries, fears, troubles, and self-pitying, all of which lead to failure, unhappiness and loss...for weakness cannot persist in a power evolving universe."[4] If all you do is react to change based on your emotions, survival will become your primary goal. Purpose provides the direction for you to make sense out of the irrational and sometimes unpredictable world in which you live.

The challenge is not to create a purpose but to discover the purpose that already exists within you. Holding tight to your purpose will produce fullness of life in spite of the multitude of events attempting to manipulate you. "There's no grander sight in the world," believed Orison Swett Marden, "than that of a person fired with a great purpose, dominated by one unwavering aim."[5]

> Successful people have a strong purpose. Strong enough to make them form the habit of doing things they don't like to do in order to accomplish the purpose they want to accomplish.
>
> Earl Nightingale[6]

Chapter 31

LOOSEN UP!
LIGHTEN UP! LIVE IT UP!

Humor is the great thing, the saving thing. The minute it crops up, all our irritations and resentments slip away, and a sunny spirit takes their place.

Mark Twain[1]

IF YOU WANT TO INCREASE the quality of your life, listen carefully and develop your sense of humor. In a *Success* magazine article entitled "Lighten Up: Stuffed Shirts Have Short Careers," Roger Ailes wrote: "The only advice some of my clients need when they come to see me can be summed up in two words: Lighten up. It's ironic, but your career can depend on whether you get serious about taking yourself less seriously."[2]

Our tendency toward a seriously stuffy, sanctimonious, sophistication toward life needs a healthy injection of infectious humor.

In a poll conducted by *Entertainment Weekly* magazine, they found that 82 percent of the people who go to movies want to laugh, 7 percent want to cry, and 3 percent want to scream.[3] I definitely fall into the 82 percent bracket. When I go to the movies, I normally scout out the comedies. Science fiction gives me a headache. Suspense makes my stomach tense. Dramas are just too depressing. But laughter producing comedies stimulate my immune system. Besides, when I'm laughing I can put the cares of the world aside because it is virtually impossible to think of anything else.

I received a call from my brother around supper time on a Friday evening. It was a call I anxiously awaited. My dad hadn't been feeling well and his doctor was running a series of tests. His iron was low, but in addition, the doctor was uncomfortable with the lumps he felt in the abdomen area.

The call confirmed my greatest fear. "I have bad news, Glenn," Joel said. "Dad has cancer." There was an uncomfortable silence, and then I asked, "When do you want me there?" It was decided I would come the next morning to be with Dad as he underwent a series of tests to confirm the doctor's suspicions and determine a plan of action.

My wife was at a women's retreat and the children were gone for the evening. *What am I going to do all night? How do I wait out the hours knowing there is nothing I can do?* I'm sure you've had that helpless feeling at one time or another.

Our community has one theater which features one movie at a time. I decided to go. For 107 minutes my mind was occupied with the humorous comments, concoctions, and content. It wasn't a particularly good movie but the humorous situations allowed me to soften, if only for a brief time, the emotional intensity I was feeling.

Over the next several days there were numerous sad, emotional, gut-wrenching times. I found myself interjecting humor at any point where it seemed the least bit appropriate. The chuckles and belly laughs eased the fear, reduced the stress, and brought comfort during some tense moments. As a family, we were able to divert our attention from the pain, fear, and curve ball life had thrown.

"I have seen what a laugh can do," Bob Hope reflected. "It can transform almost unbearable tears into something bearable, even hopeful."[4]

Laughter is a cheap medicine. It distracts your attention, changes your attitude and outlook on life, causes relaxation and reduction of tension while increasing the body's natural pain killers. In short, laughter relaxes our tensions and promotes a feeling of well-being. It allows us to take a brief sabbatical away from the serious, the pain, and the tension. The ability to laugh is a sure sign of someone living a healthy life. It is a gift we give ourselves.

Norman Cousins commented on another benefit of laughter. "I've never known a person," he said, "who possessed the gift of hearty laughter to be burdened by constipation."[5] Sounds like a beneficial outcome to me.

Humor and its sidekick laughter have a few more benefits. They are tension reducers in times of change, emotional stabilizers during adversity, creativity stimulators, and marvelous reminders to live enthusiastically. Medically speaking, we know that laughter increases endorphins. Those little guys energize us and increase our endurance.

> There ain't much fun in medicine, but there's a heck of a lot of medicine in fun.
>
> Josh Billings[6]

Section Nine

CULTIVATE A FUN SPIRIT

Chapter 32

RENEW THE CHILD IN YOU

We don't stop laughing because we grow old, we grow old because we quit laughing.

Michael Pritchard[1]

ALVIN SCHWARTZ SAID, "LAUGHTER IS the natural sound of childhood."[2] Visit your local preschool and you'll quickly agree with that statement. Reviving that childlike spirit will reap substantial adult benefits.

To be fun and have fun has proven instrumental in fostering creativity, enhancing problem-solving, and increasing retention in the classroom. An absence of fun can reduce productivity, increase job turnover, and have an acute negative impact on morale. Injecting a childlike spirit in all facets of life increases enjoyment.

Maintaining a sense of child-like behavior should be a life-long pursuit. Children too soon are told to grow up, to act like an adult. So, what do they do? Life gets heavy. Playfulness deteriorates. Problems are catastrophized. They start seeking artificial and some-times inappropriate ways to escape from the drudgery of adulthood.

Do we really want children to begin acting like adults, or would it be better for adults to recapture a bit of their childhood spirit?

I want my children to tell their friends about how much fun it was living in our home. It wasn't fun because we were childish, but we approached our relationships, mealtimes, family trips, holidays, and life in general with a spirit of joy and playfulness. Work wasn't a drudgery for Mom and Dad, but our children saw a passion for what we did. Their childhood dreams, school events, personal endeavors, difficult decisions, complicated relationships, and other activities were all viewed as opportunities to create fullness in their lives.

A child-like spirit produces creativity, fun, productivity, and a desire to get up and do it all over again tomorrow. That's why young children rarely need much prodding to get them going in the morning. Of course, once we introduce them to an alarm clock, they immediately recognize that getting up in the morning is certainly not meant to be a joyous occasion. Thus we begin one of the dreaded journeys into adulthood.

As you observe and experience life, ask yourself: "How would a preschooler respond?" This simple exercise is certain to brighten what you see. "When you discard arrogance, complexity and a few other things that can get in the way," advises the *Tao of the Pooh* author Benjamin Hoff, "sooner or later you will discover that simple, childlike and mysterious secret...Life is Fun."[3]

Look for humor everywhere you go. Create reasons for laughter, or laugh for no reason at all. Spread your sense of joy around. It will not only enrich your life but draw people closer to you and improve their lives as well.

I am well aware that the ability to laugh or see the world through humorous eyes is not for everybody. In fact, I recommend only those who want to have fun, enjoy their life, and feel alive consider such an outrageous recommendation to **lighten up...loosen up...and live it up.**

Realize that a sense of humor is deeper than laughter and more satisfying than comedy and delivers more rewards than merely being entertaining. A sense of humor sees the fun in everyday experiences. It is more important to have fun than it is to be funny.

Laurence J. Peter and Bill Dana[4]

Chapter 33

LISTEN FOR LIFE'S
LAUGHABLE MOMENTS

Everything is funny as long as it's happening to somebody else.

Will Rogers[1]

FROM THE BOARDROOM TO THE bedroom, office to the bathroom orifice, main street to the airways, life's laughable moments are everywhere. Expect the unexpected. Open your eyes to the abnormal. Let your ears hear the humor. Allow your heart to overflow with laughter. Look for at least one situation each day for which you can enjoy a hearty burst of laughter.

Looking for these laughable moments is a skill Linda Ellerbee learned to deal with the devastating news she had breast cancer. In 1992, the discovery was made and a double mastectomy ordered to save her life.

That summer Linda bought some breast prostheses to use while swimming. Instead of fastening them to her skin with Velcro as the directions instructed, she simply inserted the prostheses into her bathing suit. When she came out of the water, one had made its way around to her back. "Now," said Linda, "you can either laugh at such a thing or cry your eyes out." She decided to laugh.[2]

Ms. Ellerbee was quoted as saying, "I have always felt that laughter in the face of reality is probably the finest sound there is and will last until the day when the game is called on account of darkness. In this world, a good time to laugh is any time you can."[3]

Laughable moments occur daily. Whether you laugh or cry depends entirely on your ability to think funny, and often times, laugh at yourself. Capitalizing on the laughable moments can help you play enthusiastically, live gracefully, endure the pressures of change, and remain resilient when adversity rears its ugly head.

Laughter isn't a cure all. I've often compared it to changing a baby's dirty diaper—it isn't a permanent solution but it sure makes things better for a while.

Listen for the subtle, soft, and simple laughter moments.

> A chuckle a day may not keep the doctor away, but it sure does make those times in Life's waiting room a little more bearable.
> Anne Wilson Schaef[4]

Chapter 34

THINK FUNNY

Laughter is the most powerful state of mind there is. When you're laughing, you can't think of anything else.

H. Jackson Brown[1]

L IFE HAS A BOUNTIFUL AMOUNT of difficult and serious moments. Our job is to find responses that keep life in perspective. Begin to view your stressful experiences as a source of laughter material. Change provides bountiful reasons to be upset, worried, and confused. Find ways to laugh at the craziness and absurdity of it all.

In 1981 President Ronald Reagan was shot by a would-be assassin. As his condition was being evaluated by medical personnel, he reportedly looked up and responded, "I hope you're all Republicans."[2] His ability to think funny helped President Reagan relieve the tension of a nation concerned about his condition.

On another occasion President and Mrs. Reagan appeared on *Good Morning America*. Mrs. Reagan was close to the edge of the stage and suddenly fell off. Startled by the unexpected event, a number of people rushed over to offer assistance while the President watched.

Once he was assured she was okay, President Reagan looked over at her and said, "Nancy, I told you not to fall off the platform unless I wasn't getting any applause."[3]

It is important to remember that what we think about will determine our reactions. "Thinking funny" does not mean every event is a "ha-ha" experience. Psychological research verifies that humor is good therapy. It helps you keep life in perspective. So, "thinking funny" is a choice to see the bright side.

I remember an especially trying time during my college years (I think the trying time lasted about four years) when my roommate finally chided me, "Cheer up, things could get worse." I did cheer up and sure enough, things got worse.

Thinking funny won't keep you from getting hit by trouble and difficulties. It won't ensure that the road ahead will be void of hills and valleys, but it will give you the psychological boost you need to handle the ups and downs.

Thinking funny involves training your mind to see the light side of the dark side of life. Laugh or cry. It's a choice. Crying cleanses the tear ducts while laughter encourages the soul.

James Russell Lowell possessed a light-hearted attitude about growing old. While passing a building on the outskirts of Boston, he noticed a sign reading, "Home for Incurable Children." Turning to a friend, he remarked, "They'll get me in there some day."[4]

How about the lady experiencing a particularly frustrating round of golf. Back in the clubhouse she laments: "I finally figured out my problem. I was standing too close to the ball…after I hit it."[5]

LIGHTEN UP…THINK FUNNY!

> Sometimes you just need to look reality in the eye, and deny it.
> Garrison Keillor[6]

Chapter 35

BE WILLING TO LAUGH
AT YOURSELF

If I were given the opportunity to present a gift to the next generation it would be the ability for each individual to learn to laugh at himself.

Charles Schultz[1]

ONE OF THE MOST LIBERATING experiences of life is to be able to laugh at yourself," Dr. John Maxwell says. "When you lose that ability, everything in life takes on a much too serious complexion. I've discovered that a lot of my idiosyncrasies can either be a cause for despair or hilarity. I've decided to choose the latter. Life is strangely funny if you don't have your value or sense of adequacy tied up in being perfect."[2]

"Humor is an attitude, a way of looking at the world," says humor expert Joel Goodman. "Laughter is a way of expressing humor."[3] How do you see your world? How do you express it? Can the people closest to you recognize how much you love life by your ability to laugh at yourself?

G.K. Chesterton spoke to the sourpusses of this world when he wrote, "Madmen are always serious; they go mad from lack of humor."[4] Maybe that's why I admire guys like the vertically challenged (short) wanna-be cowboy who quit wearing cowboy boots. He kidded others that the boots gave him a rash … under his armpits. This attitude reflects the most refined sense of humor—the ability to laugh at ourselves.

I've been bald for many years. I know every bald joke there is, yet there is always somebody who wants to share a bit of their jocular wisdom with me:

> Grass doesn't grow on busy streets.

> Bald in the front, you're a thinker. Bald in the back, you're a lover. Bald all over, you only think you're a lover.

> God only covers that which he doesn't like.

> I may have lost the waves, but I still have the beach.[5]

I'm sure you've heard them all as well. You know what? I laugh every time someone decides to entertain me with these worn out, overused, clichés. Why? Why not? I like to laugh. It sure beats crawling in a corner and lamenting my follicle challenge.

Think of all the failures, stumbling blocks, embarrassing moments, and down-right stupid things you've experienced. Now recall how six months later, you laughed about them (or should have). John Powell observed: "Blessed is He who has learned to laugh at himself, for he shall never cease to be entertained."[6]

One final word of encouragement and admonition from Ethel Barrymore. "You grow up," she said, "on the day you have the first real laugh—at yourself."[7]

> We're only young once, but with humor, we can be immature forever.
>
> Art Gliner[8]

Section Ten

SEEK NEW HORIZONS

Chapter 36

Notice Opportunities

Too often the opportunity knocks, but by the time you disengage the chain, push back the bolt, unhook the two locks and shut off the burglar alarms, it's too late.

Rita Cooledge[1]

JACK WELCH, FORMER CEO OF General Electric, encourages us to, "Stimulate and relish change. Don't be frightened or paralyzed by it. See change as an opportunity, not just a threat."[2]

If you see change as a threat, there is a tendency to become defensive, irrational, and prone to discouragement. Finger pointing, blaming, and complaining become the order of the day. People go home drained and discouraged because their energies are spent on fighting the perceived negative impact of change. As a result, hundreds of opportunities are lost because their focus is blurred, causing them to be blind to positive possibilities.

If, on the other hand, change is viewed as an opportunity, you set in motion constructive behavior that can make change your ally. Every situation you encounter can become an opportunity. Excitement is the prerequisite to uncovering possibilities and generating options. Energy is multiplied when passion becomes a part of the formula.

When change is happening all around you, stop and re-examine where you are going and what you are encountering. Learn to draw out of life's events valuable nuggets leading you to golden opportunities. Greek philosopher Plutarch wrote, "As bees extract honey from thyme, the strongest and driest of herbs, so sensible men often get advantage and profit from the most awkward circumstances."[3]

Roy Speer and Lowell Paxson capitalized on their observations of people's lifestyles. They found: 1. People like to shop. 2. People like to watch TV. 3. People like to shop or watch TV anytime they please. These simple conclusions led to the development of The Home Shopping Network, Inc., a 24-hour TV shopping channel. Speaking of extracting honey, this little venture appealed to TV watchers and shoppers everywhere, generating hundreds of millions of dollars in revenue annually.[4]

This opportunistic approach led Walt Disney to reinvent the amusement park. With it, Ted Turner revolutionized cable television; Colonel Sanders helped launch a multi-billion dollar fast food industry; Bill Gates catapulted to computer software stardom; and Sam Walton created his "always the low price" Walmart shopping experience.

Being prepared to capitalize on opportunities is an ongoing venture. There is no such thing as attaining and resting. We are constantly determining what we need next to remain effective. Invest in some reflection time. Reappraise your learning curve. What resources have you accessed? Are there untapped energy reserves?

Ask yourself: *What presently works for me that I need to continue doing to create the ideal future? What elements of my present and past need to be discarded? What excess baggage hinders me from achieving and experiencing what I want in life?* Snakes shed their skin as they outgrow it. People need to shed themselves of habits that have outlived their usefulness or inhibit the pursuit of new possibilities. "Equilibrium is death," said Kevin Kelly. "Seek persistent equilibrium."[5] Therein exists the entrance to a refreshing and expanded view of change.

Expect to strain a little. Straining and stretching increase our flexibility. Doing only what comes easily or naturally gets us nowhere, and more than likely produces little more than treading water or even losing ground.

Heed the words of Alexander Graham Bell: "When one door closes, another one opens. But we look so long and regretfully upon the closed door that we do not see the one that has opened for us."[6]

> You create your own opportunities out of the same raw materials from which other people create their defeats.
>
> Bernie Siegel M.D.[7]

Chapter 37

MOVE BOLDLY INTO THE UNKNOWN

To risk is to loosen your grip on the known and the certain,
and to reach for something you are not entirely sure of but you
believe is better than what you now have, or is at least necessary
to survive. Taking a risk is central to everything worthwhile
in life. Without taking a risk, no one finds true love, no one
develops real power, and no one gains prestige. Everything you
really want in life involves taking a risk.

David Viscott[1]

AKIO MORITA AND ANOTHER MAN started a new company
called Tokyo Telecommunications Engineering in a
bombed-out department store in Tokyo.

Ten years later, the company introduced the world to the first
transistor radio. An American company, Bulova, knew opportunity
when they saw it and offered to buy the radios at a tempting profit.
Mr. Morita hesitated to accept the offer because the radios would be
sold under the Bulova name.[2]

According to a 1994 *USA Today* article entitled "Sony's Legend
Stepping Down," Morita wanted to establish his own company's

brand name.[3] So even though the deal would have brought his strug-gling company an infusion of much needed cash, Morita decided against the deal, informing the executives at Bulova, "I am now taking the first step for the next fifty years of my company."

Morita's bold move helped his company to become one of the greatest success stories in business. They introduced the world to such innovative products as the VCR and compact disc players. Today, they have diversified into a number of products and busi-ness ventures and their name is synonymous with innovation and quality. Remember Mr. Morita's decision to forego the sure thing by risking his future every time you see the brand name "Sony."[2]

"It is our destiny to move out," said Louis L'Amour, "to accept the challenge, to dare the unknown..."[4] This advice tends to unsettle human nature. Akio Morita's experience is an example of one who defied the pull of an inviting offer to reach for something that wasn't a sure thing. How about you? Rather than accepting security by knowing what tomorrow will bring, or the boredom of knowing what the day after tomorrow will bring, how about moving boldly in the direction of adventurous living.

The story is told of a spy who was captured and sentenced to death by a general in the Persian army. Before execution, the general would engage in a rather unusual procedure. He would offer the captor a choice between the firing squad or a big, black door.

The spy was surprised at the offer and deliberated on his choice for a long time until finally deciding on the firing squad. Moments later, his life was over.

The general turned to his aide and said, "They always prefer the known to the unknown. Yet, we give them a choice."[5]

The aide himself was unaware of what consequences exist beyond the big, black door so he asked his commander. "Freedom," replied the general, "and I've only known a few brave enough to take it."

How comfortable and almost automatic it is to become preoc-cupied with the familiar and satisfied with what is. Leaving the security blanket behind and venturing into the unknown is scary yet continually playing it safe is boring. We need a balance, an expanded menu of options that tempt our taste buds.

It's a test to let go and enjoy whatever potentialities this day will bring. I understand how chancy it is for people to leap outside the box of status quo. Fortunately, I'm learning how exciting it can be to expose yourself to the unknown—not recklessly but with calculated enthusiasm, so that you can enjoy the possibilities. Some of the things that I enjoy the most now are things that I was initially fearful of trying, simply because I didn't want to appear clumsy, inept, or uneducated. This isn't really taking a chance; it's giving yourself a chance to test your limits, to prove what you can do even in a world that seems crazy.

To get started, follow the advice of Virgil Thomson who said, "Try a thing you haven't done three times. Once, to get over the fear of doing it. Twice, to learn how to do it. And a third time to figure out whether you like it or not."[6]

Are you primed to try out some wild ideas? How about breaking out of your old routines and doing something different. Extend yourself. Put some adventure in your approach to handling things instead of relying on conventional means. Give yourself permission to explore, to move forward without the guarantee of success. You can't really avoid risk, so why not stretch yourself and see what opportunities you've been ignoring? The worst that can happen is that you won't get what you're accustomed to getting.

Will the fear go away? Probably not. Dr. Susan Jeffries observed, "As long as I continue to push out into the world, as long as I continue to stretch my capabilities, as long as I continue to take risks in making my dreams come true, I am going to experience fear."[7] There will be a recurring fear of failing or embarrassment. The fear of rejection, uncertainty, and disappointment will rear their ugly heads. Even the fear of difficulty will threaten. The desire for safety will continually tempt you to stop where you are and rely on old faithful. Don't let it get to you.

Thoughts to enhance your risk-taking:

1. Other people have been where you're thinking of going. Let that knowledge inspire your spirit to take the journey.

2. It can't be that bad. Ask yourself: "What have I got to lose?" Accept the fact that you won't necessarily like or succeed at everything you try but you'll undoubtedly learn a lot. If you can handle the worst possible outcome, take the risk.

3. You can do it! Bruce Barton said, "Nothing splendid has ever been achieved except by those who dared believe that something inside them was superior to circumstances."[8] There is a direct correlation between your self-image and risk quotient. Break through your self-constructed ceiling of limitations and realize you can progress past where you are. Challenge your self-doubts and you'll grow stronger.

4. No matter what, you will benefit. Risk takers who win or lose learn to focus on the process as well as the results. They learn to rise above what doesn't work and find another way to be successful. They see possibilities and opportunities that propel them past the status quo and mediocrity. They experience the challenge of sacrifice and the satisfaction of solutions.

"The world is full of wonders, riches, powers, puzzles," said Toni Flores. "What it holds can make us horrified, sorrowful, amazed, confused, joyful. But nothing can make us bored. Boredom is the result of some pinch in ourselves, not of some lack in the world."[9] Boredom is the unconscious friend of those who fail to experience the world's wonders. Don't become so caught up in your small world that you fail to take advantage of opportunities available to you. Allow security to remain a stranger and risk to become your friend.

> Living at risk is jumping off the cliff and building your wings on the way down.
>
> Ray Bradbury[10]

Chapter 38

THE FUN IS IN THE CHALLENGE

You can always tell when you are on the road to success; it's uphill all the way.

Paul Harvey[1]

TOM MONAGHAN WAS BORN IN Ann Arbor, Michigan in 1937. His father died when Tom was four-years-old. He grew up in foster homes, orphanages, and finally a detention home for delinquent children. He attempted to pursue his childhood dream of becoming a priest but was kicked out of seminary, forcing him to look at other career options. After a short stint at Ferris State College, Monaghan ran out of money and enlisted in the Marine Corps.

During his transition back to civilian life, Monaghan's brother suggested they buy a pizza parlor call Dominick's in Ypsilanti. Tom borrowed the money and became an instant entrepreneur. The years that followed were very challenging. His brother wanted out of the partnership. A new partner embezzled enough money to leave Monaghan broke, and he was forced to change the name of the company to Domino's. His original store burned. Domino's went public, resulting in near financial collapse, and then the Domino's sugar people sued him for infringing on their name. A five year, $1.5 million dollar fight won him the right to maintain Domino's as his company's name. Hundred's of stores were added to the Domino's chain and Monaghan amassed a fortune.[2]

Tom Monaghan's character was revealed in a visit he persisted in setting up with his idol Ray Kroc, founder of McDonald's. Kroc grilled him with questions about his operation and then leaned forward in his chair and said, "I'm going to give you some advice. You have made it now. You can do anything you want; make all the money you can possibly spend. So what I think you should do now is slow down. Take it easy. Open a few stores every year, but be very careful. Play it safe."

Monaghan was dumbfounded. How could his entrepreneurial hero suggest such a thing? Finally he blurted out, "But that wouldn't be any fun!"

A brief moment of silence seemed like an eternity and then Kroc smiled and responded, "That's just what I hoped you would say!"[3]

Struggles, challenges, dreams, obstacles, and setbacks are all a part of the fun and satisfaction on the road to success. Only those intent on making the journey as enjoyable as the destination can endorse such a courageous pursuit.

> If you wish success in life, make perseverance your bosom friend, experience your wise counselor, caution your elder brother and hope your guardian genius.
>
> Joseph Addison[4]

Chapter 39

TOO FAT TO FLY

Progress is a tide. If we stand still we will surely be drowned. To
stay on the crest, we have to keep moving.

Harold Mayfield[1]

INNOVATORS, ENTREPRENEURS, AND ADVENTURE SEEKERS all
know the road ahead is filled with uncertainties. If they waited
for the conditions to be perfect, they would never pursue their
dreams. They are also keenly aware how quickly atrophy sets in if
they are not constantly moving toward their goals.

The great Danish philosopher, Soren Kierkegaard, once told a
story of a flock of geese that was starting to head South to escape
the blast of wintry winds. The first night they landed in a farmer's
yard and filled themselves with corn. Next morning they flew on—
all, that is, except one. "The corn is good," this big goose said, "so
I will stay and enjoy it another day." The next morning he decided
to wait still another day, and another after that, enjoying the delicious food. Pretty soon he had developed a habit. "Tomorrow I will
fly South," he said.

Then came the inevitable day when the winds of winter were so severe that waiting longer would mean death in the frozen wastes. So he stretched his wings and waddled across the barnyard, picking up speed as he went. But alas! He was too fat to fly. He had waited too long.[2]

Enjoying the fruits of past labors. Coming upon unexpected satisfying experiences. Achieving a personal goal. Making a huge sale. Getting that long awaited promotion. These types of experiences tend to create two opposing reactions. Some people develop a greater passion for action and a desire to outdo what they did before. Still others become so comfortable a severe case of stagnation sets in. Those who spend too long enjoying what they do without maintaining a steady diet of action will soon find themselves stale, disinterested, and unprepared to face the next challenge.

Remember this: untalented, mediocre people who fully apply themselves go further than the superior people who don't. Since each positive, progressive action you take propels you closer to desirable rewards and outcomes, the sooner you begin, the better.

Thomas Edison was right. "Everything comes to he who hustles while he waits."[3] It's not what you're going to do when things start going your way, but it's what you're doing now.

> Success is not the result of spontaneous combustion. You must set yourself on fire.
>
> Reggie Leach[4]

Section Eleven

GO FOR IT!

Chapter 40

RESIST COMPLACENCY

I've felt that dissatisfaction is the basis of progress. When we
become satisfied in business, we become obsolete.

J. Willard Marriott Sr.[1]

MR. MARRIOTT'S COMMENT ABOUT BUSINESS has a direct
correlation to people. Pablo Casals, the great cellist, was
asked why, at eight-five years of age, he continued to
practice five hours a day. He replied, "Because I think I'm getting
better."[2] Without a fervent desire to grow, it is possible to become a
victim of our own success.

Complacency can be a terrible disease that spreads throughout
all areas of our life. It attacks when we're savoring our achievements
and convincing ourselves that success is forever. Suddenly, we are
aghast at how terrible we feel when we realize success's guarantee
of longevity has run out. Failure comes knocking at the door. As Joe
Paterno said, "The minute you think you've got it made, disaster is
just around the corner."[3]

Thomas Edsion believed that, "Restlessness is discontent—and
discontent is the first necessity of progress. Show me a thoroughly

satisfied man—and I will show you a failure."[4] Continuing hunger and restlessness is fine. I applaud it. The unguarded pursuit of more money, more recognition, increased status, peer approval or whatever measures we use to determine success is not. These fleeting mementos of success can rapidly disappear, but living successfully can continually be renewed.

Creative discontent will forge you ahead. Stubborn selfishness impedes progress. Life needs balance.

American broadcast journalist, Barbara Walters, knows success. In her climb up the ladder, she commented: "Success can make you go one of two ways. It can make you a prima donna, or it can smooth the edges, take away the insecurities, let the nice things come out."[5] This challenge for balance requires considerable effort, determination, self-discipline and a clear understanding of what success means to us.

When success is viewed as a continuum of growth in our spiritual maturity, professional fulfillment, emotional well-being, relationship development, financial management, and mental expansion, there is little room for complacency. Based on this success paradigm, I cherish times spent with successful people. Witnessing their progress on the success journey generates excitement about the possibilities in my life. You need not, and should not, compare your achievements or life with other people but use them as a model to elevate yourself. Notice how winners rarely back away from opportunities to grow and expand their vision. Feel the spirit that drives them toward their dreams. Pay close attention to the lifestyle of a winner and consider how you might seize the future for yourself.

Always remember this: If you want to get to the top of the ladder of success, you must begin on the bottom rung. It's congested down there. In fact, one of the toughest obstacles you'll face on the way up the success continuum is the traffic jam caused by the crowd who are complacent with their growth. Don't let them distract you. Keep climbing, growing, reaching to become and experience everything this great life has to offer.

The rung of a ladder was never meant to rest upon, but merely to hold a person's foot long enough to enable that individual to put the other foot somewhat higher.

Thomas Huxley[6]

Chapter 41

EXERCISE YOUR MIND

The best cure for a sluggish mind is to disturb its routine.
William Danforth[1]

A TEAM OF PRODUCT DEVELOPERS AT Campbell Soup Company got together for a brainstorming session. The group began by randomly selecting the word "handle" from a dictionary. Through free association, someone suggested the word "utensil." This led to "fork." One participant joked about a soup that could be eaten with a fork. The team reasoned that you couldn't eat soup with a fork unless it was thick with vegetables and meat—and Campbell's Chunky Soups, an extremely successful product line, was born.[2]

There is nothing mystical about creativity. People tend to think that creativity is reserved for a select few and the rest of us will remain void of any innovative birthright. Nothing could be further from the truth. Below are a few practical ways to stimulate your creative juices. Relax. Let your mind go and enjoy the journey into creative problem solving, idea development, or product ingenuity.

1. Think Fresh. R. Buckminster Fuller was a man of many talents. His adult life was spent as an inventor, engineer, architect, poet, and star-gazer. "Bucky," as his friends referred to him, was most importantly a creative thinker. He was responsible for the invention, development, and implementation of over one hundred seventy patented ideas. He authored twenty-four books and made fifty-seven trips around the world sharing his abundant supply of ideas with others.

As a young non-conforming student, Fuller was expelled from Harvard in his freshman year. His enthusiasm and creativity remained undampened. Fuller would spend up to twenty-two hours a day studying math, architecture, and physics. His self-attained knowledge combined with his creative ideas made him a man ahead of his time and the leading innovator of futuristic products. In fact, he was often branded an eccentric because his ideas seemed so impossible at the time. However, the put-downs and criticism had little effect on Bucky and he continued to create, design, and invent up until his death.

R. Buckminister Fuller became one of the greatest innovators of this century.[3] His creative genius stemmed from this simple yet profound thought: "People should think things out fresh and not just accept conventional terms and the conventional way of doing things."[4]

Murray Spangler developed a mind set recommended by "Bucky" Fuller. As a department store janitor, Spangler suffered considerable discomfort from the dust his broom stirred. The wheezing and coughing prompted him to find an "unconventional" way to clean floors.

"Why not eliminate the sweeping," he thought, "and suck up the dust instead." His friend, H.W. Hoover, financed the first awkward but functional vacuum cleaner. Spangler's futuristic, uncluttered thinking allowed him to overcome personal discomfort and go beyond conventional thinking.[5]

Unconventional thinkers, people who exercise their brains, tend to stumble on to great discoveries in their pursuit of unique ideas. In 1953, a rocket chemical company chemist persisted in developing a water replacement formula. On his fortieth attempt, he was successful in creating a substance used in 79 percent of American homes.

According to *USA Today*, the product is used to loosen toes stuck in bathtub faucets; cure mange in dogs; get stuck fingers out of pop bottles; make fish bait more attractive; loosen rusted nuts and bolts; get a burglar out of a vent pipe; quiet squeaking wheels and springs; loosen arthritic knees and elbows.

The product? Think about it. Water displacement. Forty attempts. It's WD-40®. The famous blue and yellow can contains a product that comes in handy in a multitude of unconventional emergencies.[6]

2. Expand Your Current Thinking. Pablo Picasso endorsed a revolutionary approach to creativity. One day, he was standing outside his house looking around the yard. A rusty old bicycle resting against the porch caught his attention. Picasso focused on the metal frame of the bike and noticed the handle bars resembled the horns of a bull. Removing the handle bars from the bike, he proceeded to his studio and created a sculpture of a charging bull. Picasso tapped his creative imagination to turn the ordinary into something dramatic. Picasso's creative success was attributed to the ability of expanding on one theme to create another.[7]

Later in his life, Picasso shared the secret for escaping tunnel vision. "Every act of creation is first of all an act of destruction," preached Picasso.[8] One must first break down the barriers of present limitations, restrictive thoughts, and old habits that strangle our creative efforts. Then and only then can our creative genius be explored.

3. Challenge Established Rules. Creativity expert, Roger Von Oech, says "Challenging the established rules is necessary to awaken our creativity." Von Oech tells how in the winter of 333 B.C., the Macedonian general Alexander and his army arrived in the Asian city of Gordium to spend the winter. Alexander is told about the legend surrounding the town's famous knot, the "Gordian Knot." According to local prophecy, whoever is able to untie this exceptionally complex knot will become king of Asia. Alexander is fascinated by the local legend and asks to be shown the knot so he can attempt to untie it. He studies the strangely tied rope and makes numerous fruitless attempts to locate the rope's end.[9]

Unscathed by his failure to unfasten the knot, he approached the challenge using Picasso's advice. Alexander pulled out his sword and sliced the knot in half...thereby inheriting control of Asia.

4. Get Crazy. Creative people are constantly on the lookout for breakthrough ideas. They recreate and rearrange the present by finding novel ways to approach specific problems. They use their creativity to find new solutions (sometimes by using unrelated ideas as they fit the present situation). Many times the seemingly craziest ideas become the most successful. While this approach tends to invite criticism, creative thinkers continue to think things out fresh, knowing that novel ideas often solve complex problems.

Novel ideas will produce criticism from the masses, but Everett M. Rogers suggests that, "When 5 percent of society accepts an idea, it becomes imbedded in the population. When 20 percent agrees, it's unstoppable."[10] Even the unstoppable get criticized.

"You can't put an alligator on a shirt to replace the pocket. Nobody will buy them!"

"You want to sell me a chicken recipe? You'll never get this idea off the ground Colonel Sanders!"

"Mr. Bell, please remove that silly toy from my office. There is no room in the market for a telephone."

"How dumb do you think I am? You can't put music on scotch tape."

The history books are full of people who realized creativity begins with destroying perceived limitations and remaining untouched by criticism.

5. Search For New Possibilities. Einstein represented the best of creative thinkers when he observed: "To raise new questions, new possibilities, to regard old problems from a new angle requires creative imagination."[11] Creativity emerges out of personal commitment to raise new questions, explore new possibilities, focus on old problems from a new angle, and be willing to implement ideas that may not be in tune with the normally accepted way of doing things.

Charles Darrow was a salesperson living during the Great Depression who must have been an advocate of Einstein's thinking. When the sales positions ceased, he squeezed out a living walking dogs, washing cars, and other assorted odd jobs. In the evening, he worked on developing a board game that several people could play at once. Darrow had visions of every home owning one of his games.

The first company to purchase his idea sold five thousand games in the first year. Parker Brothers later purchased the game, beefed up the marketing, and today, twenty thousand of these games are sold every week.

Darrows' willingness to pursue new possibilities resulted in America's favorite board game—Monopoly.[12]

How about the young salesperson asked by the Hookless Fastener Company how to increase the sale of zippers. He suggested they replace the buttons on the front of men's pants with zippers. This unconventional idea was almost scrapped. A trial run took this non-traditional idea from skepticism to a standard in the clothing industry.[13]

A discussion on new possibilities from fresh thinking wouldn't be complete without considering George de Mestral. While brushing burrs out of his wool pants and his dog's coat, de Mestral became curious about the tenacity of the burrs. Concentrated observation of the burrs under a microscope revealed hundreds of tiny hooks snagged in mats of wool and fur. Years later, he made a connection and the invention of Velcro fasteners was born.[14] George de Mestral considered an old problem with new eyes. He raised new questions and sought new possibilities. Einstein would have been proud.

Dr. Michael LeBoeuf advises: "Don't let other people define your creative potential. No one, including you, knows what you're capable of doing or thinking up."[15]

In a three-month creativity study, psychologists researched the characteristics of creative people. Education, family backgrounds, and a variety of personal preferences were all considered as possible variables. In the end, one single common factor was found to determine an individual's creativity—attitude. Simply stated, creative people think they are creative and vice versa.

Creative potential is one of the great God-given tools available to us. The extent to which we develop this gift depends on our attitude towards it. No one knows for sure what they're capable of and therein lies the excitement.

Innovators don't always invent new radical ideas. Instead, they are careful observers of the world around them. They borrow and rethink existing ideas to solve problems and create unexposed opportunities. Nurture originality and new frontiers will be discovered.

> Some painters transform the sun into a yellow spot; others transform a yellow spot into the sun.
>
> Pablo Picasso[16]

Chapter 42

WHAT'S YOUR SECRET, MR. SMITH?

Our souls are not hungry for fame, comfort, wealth, or power.
Those rewards create almost as many problems as they solve.
Our souls are hungry for meaning, for the sense that we have
figured out how to live so that our lives matter, so that the
world will at least be a little bit different for our having passed
through it.

Harold Kushner[1]

THE *TODAY SHOW'S* WILLARD SCOTT had a memorable interview one morning with a Mr. Smith, who was celebrating his 102nd birthday. Unique to this interview were the props that accompanied Mr. Smith. Willard was having a difficult time getting Mr. Smith to focus on the interview instead of the potted chrysanthemums and orchids that surrounded him.

"Mr. Smith," Willard repeated, "we'd all like to know to what you attribute your long life." Mr. Smith, sharp as a tack, continued to draw attention to his flowers. "This little lovely won't bloom for another two years," he informed the television viewing audience. As Mr. Smith touched the flowers, sprayed them with water, and gazed upon their beauty, Willard made another attempt to discover the man's secret for living 102 years. "What's your secret for living so long and staying alive?"

The old man quickly replied with a question of his own: "Who would take care of these beautiful flowers?" This wasn't exactly what Willard Scott was looking for, but Mr. Smith communicated a powerful message.[2]

Richard Gaylord Briley suggested, "If all you do is react to what this unpredictable, irrational world throws at you, lacking positive plans and purposes of your own to give direction to your life, your life has no rational purpose beyond mere survival."[3] The 102-year-old Mr. Smith was more interested in the purpose that provided passion in his life than the mere fact that he had "survived" for more than a century. He had learned how to put life in his living rather than just adding years to his life.

Don't make this philosophical. Present in each of us is a reason for living waiting to be discovered. To be committed and working for a valuable purpose, a purpose larger than your self interest, is one of the secrets of making life significant. Identifying and aligning with a purpose adds meaning, stability, and direction to life.

I often think about an experience Supreme Court Justice Oliver Wendell Holmes had preparing to board a train. Apparently, Holmes had misplaced his ticket and was desperately searching to find it to avoid missing his train. The conductor sensed Holmes frustration and said, "Your Honor, if you do not find your ticket, you can simply mail it to the railroad. We know and trust you."

Holmes quickly replied, "I am not so concerned about your getting my ticket. I just want to know where I am going."[4] There are a lot of people wanting to know where they are going in life.

Purposeless people are like the Jacana, a unique tropical bird. It has spindly legs with long protruding toes enabling it to skip along floating weeds or, stroll across lily pads. Bird enthusiasts commonly refer to the Jacana as a "lily-trotter." Here's a bird capable of soaring through the heavens who has settled for lazily moving from flower to flower.

What a waste! Yet, there are people who drift along through life skipping from one thing to the next. They've not yet realized there are fabulous adventures and new heights waiting for them to experience once they leave their "lily-trotter" existence.

George Bernard Shaw shared this reflection:

> This is the true joy in life, being used for a purpose recognized by yourself as a mighty one. Being a force of nature instead of a feverish, selfish little clod of ailments and grievances complaining that the world will not devote itself to making you happy. I am of the opinion that my life belongs to the whole community and as I live it is my privilege—my privilege to do for it whatever I can. I want to be thoroughly used up when I die, for the harder I work the more I love. I rejoice in life for its own sake. Life is no brief candle to me; it is a sort of splendid torch which I've got a hold of for the moment and I want to make it burn as brightly as possible before handing it on to future generations.[5]

If you were to look back on your wonderful, fantastic life, what would have made it so great? What does your life stand for? What is the "why" of your life? What makes living worthwhile and meaningful regardless of the challenges you experience?

> No individual has any right to come into the world and go out of it without leaving behind him distinct and legitimate reasons for having passed through it.
>
> George Washington Carver[6]

Chapter 43

Success Is Just Around the Corner

Never give up then, for that is just the place and time that the tide will turn.

Harriet Beecher Stowe[1]

WALTER PAYTON IS CONSIDERED ONE of the great professional running backs of all time. During a Monday night football game between the New York Giants and Chicago Bears, the announcers were showering Payton with accolades. "Just think," one announcer observed, "he has accumulated over nine miles in career rushing yardage." Another announcer quickly responded, "Yeah, and that's with someone knocking him down every 4.6 yards!"[2]

"In life or in football," Rush Limbaugh observed, "touchdowns rarely take place in seventy-yard increments. Usually it's three yards and a cloud of dust."[3] Walter Payton raised a few clouds of dust. He knows that everyone—even the best—gets knocked down. The key to success is to get up and run harder the next time. It's called perseverance, tenacity, courage.

Tenacity is that wonderful quality that keeps writers writing, artists painting, athletes competing, the rest of us keeping on keeping on. Successful people persevere even when they are told that they will never make it. Malcolm Forbes, editor-in-chief of *Forbes* magazine and one of the wealthiest people in America, didn't make the staff of his college paper when he was a student at Princeton.[4]

Walt Disney had a dream that would alter the entertainment industry. He went bankrupt two or three times, had equipment repossessed, experienced a nervous breakdown, and begged for additional dollars until finally things smoothed out for him in the late 1960s. Imbedded in every Disney creation is a history of incredible tenacity and perseverance displayed by Walt Disney in the face of disheartening calamities.[5] Maybe he had heard the words of singer Ella Fitzgerald. "Just don't give up trying to do what you really want to do. Where there is love and inspiration, I don't think you can go wrong."[6]

Your level of persistence in the midst of difficulty, obstacles, and adversity is an accurate gauge of your belief in yourself. Successful people understand the necessity of coming face to face with life's undesirable situations, reaching deep inside, gathering their confidence and unhesitantly stepping forward. They do not give in or give up. There is no second-guessing. They understand the journey will produce mental and physical fatigue, but they are not about to surrender. In fact, they fully expect to pay a handsome price for the achievements they attain. In a book of letters to his young adult son titled *Mark My Words*, Canadian businessman G. Kingsley Ward writes: "No one I know of has ever experienced one success after another without defeats, failures, and disappointments, and frustrations galore along the way. Learning to overcome these times of agony is what separates the winners from the losers."[7]

Alex Haley wanted to be a writer, yet he spent much of his time in the Navy writing tedious reports and letters. That wasn't the type of writing he had in mind but such responsibilities did help refine his written communication skills.[8] After serving his country, he kept writing and writing and writing but experienced rejection upon rejection. Maybe becoming a published author just wasn't meant to be. Then came a little different rejection, not the normal form letter, but an encouraging note from an editor that said, "Nice try."

That simple note reinsured this struggling writer and offered what he viewed as a ray of hope. Finally, after many persistent years, he penned a book that has richly affected the world. The now-world-famous-author's book *Roots* was made into a television miniseries enjoyed by millions.[9]

"Hold your head high, stick your chest out," said Reverend Jesse Jackson. "You can make it. It gets dark sometimes but morning comes."[10] Morning does come and success is normally just around the corner. If only people wouldn't stop in the middle of adversity street to lament their condition. Success is waiting, but it only greets the persistent traveler.

> Persistence is what makes the impossible possible, the possible likely, and likely definite.
>
> Robert Half[11]

TAKE CHARGE OF YOUR FUTURE

Chapter 44

LIFE IS LIFE

Our limited perspective, our hopes and fears become our measure of life, and when circumstances don't fit our ideas, they become our difficulties.

Benjamin Franklin[1]

HOW CAN WE REALLY STAY calm in this crazy world? Well, I live under a simple set of operating principles that naturally contribute to ongoing positive mental health. What you are about to read is not profound, but it is important: *Life is life*.

Life is not good. Life is not bad. Life is life. It contains positive experiences as well as unwanted ones. Life awaits me fresh each day with possibilities and obstacles. At the conclusion of my day I often reflect on the learning I've experienced and the periodic pain I needed to endure. Life is life.

At the core of being uptight with life is our unwillingness to accept life for what it is, even when it occurs different from our expectations. To maintain a healthy perspective we would do well to understand Abraham Maslow's seven requirements for mental health:[2]

1. Take responsibility for your own feelings, including your happiness. Never give ownership or control of your feelings to someone else. When you refuse to acknowledge the fact that your feelings are yours and no one else's, only you are deceived and injured.

2. Give up the luxury of blaming others for your shortcomings, disappointments, and suffering. When you evaluate all of the good things that happen in your life, who is responsible? Now reflect on the shortcomings, disappointments, and suffering. Who caused them? How easy it is to take the credit for positive outcomes and pass off responsibility for what we don't like to someone else. Is that fair?

The day we stop making excuses and declare ourselves accountable is the day we can begin bringing closure and start dumping the emotional garbage of the past.

3. Face the consequences, even when the things you attempt and the risks you take bring about the worst possible results. Two-time Pulitzer Prize winner Barbara Tuchman said, "Taking responsibility for your behavior, your expenditures and your actions and not forever supposing that society must forgive you because it's 'not your fault' is the quality most needed in the next century."[3]

4. Seek to discover all of the inner resources that are available to you, even though self-discovery is at times painful and demanding. It takes courage to unveil the true feelings we have of ourselves. When you recognize the talents you possess, values you endorse, and the attitudes that shape your life, you're in a position to focus on improving yourself and reaching your potential.

5. Act on your own feelings, rather than on the approval of others—even if this means conflict at times with those who are important to you. Thomas Jefferson once said, "In matters of taste, swim in the current; in matters of principle, stand like a rock."[4] Flexibility, the ability to go with the flow, is an admirable personality trait unless it violates character. Compromised values will disintegrate your integrity. Act on your belief in what is right.

6. Take responsibility for letting go of your own negativity, including letting yourself and other people off the hook. That which we consistently think about expands. Letting go of negativity requires the disposing of negative input. Fill the thoughts of your mind and emotions in your heart with that which builds you up. Refuse to think about, dwell on, or be influenced by the mass of negative information fighting to saturate your life. Let it go! Also, release the negative judgments of others that haunt your mind.

7. Have compassion and empathy for yourself and for others, recognizing that having compassion is a very healing process. Learn to be a nice person. Be respectful. Listen to people. Find out what's important to others. Uphold people's dignity. Add joy to their lives. Accept others for who they are. Give up criticizing. Be genuinely interested in the lives of other people. Life becomes infinitely more positive when we have compassion and empathy for people.

Life is life. But it inevitably returns to us what we invest in it. Decide what you want from life and begin putting in what you're hoping to reap from life.

> True maturity only comes when you finally realize that no one is coming to the rescue.
>
> Author Unknown[5]

Chapter 45

CHOOSE YOUR RESPONSE

Too many people fear change. They cling to the familiar old shoe even if it cuts off circulation to their toes.

Wally "Famous" Amos[1]

THOSE ADAPTING WELL TO CHANGING times like these have a changeless character that provides a foundation from which they make choices to deal effectively with a vastly changing world. A spirit of innovation and personal growth allow them to adapt, accept, and even embrace the changes around them without violating their personal principles.

We can't deny the nature of our changing culture or avoid it. Change unfolds unknown variables in our lives and plans. Resist the temptation to go about your daily business blind to the unpredictable. Just because you "keep doing what you're doing" does not necessarily mean you'll keep getting what you've been getting. Actually, denial and business as usual is bound to produce less than satisfying results.

There is a courthouse in Ohio that stands in a unique location. When it rains, the rain that falls on the north side of the roof drains into Lake Ontario and flows into the Gulf of St. Lawrence. Rain falling on the south side ends up in the Mississippi River and ultimately ends up in the Gulf of Mexico.

The destiny of those raindrops can be altered by a gentle breeze or sudden gust of wind and will make a difference of more than two thousand miles in their final destination. The raindrops don't have a choice in their final destination. You do.

You have at your disposal exactly what you need to gain confidence in dealing with the winds of change. The strongest principle for determining your ultimate destination lies in the choices you make.

In response to life's events, you make two choices. First, you choose one course of action or mental response. By so doing, we are not choosing the opposite response. If you choose to proactively deal with circumstances, you are making a decision not to allow the circumstances to control you. You'll create internal resiliency and outward productivity.

And second, you must choose to give an honest effort to make that action or response a reality. This normally requires you to move out of your comfort zone into the unknown. That requires a willingness to risk discomfort, face challenges head on, and draw on your resources to make the best of every situation.

This is critical always, but especially in days like these! As Gloria Estefan beautifully sings: "We seal our fate with the choices we make."[2] We control the choices we make and then the choices control us.

It is important to invest our energies in things over which we have control versus no control issues. Many people find it easier to focus on, worry about, and complain about things outside their control. Why? It doesn't take any effort. Many people don't want to act, they want to whine and fret. Action takes too much work.

Remember, you can't always control what happens to you in life. Sometimes you can, sometimes you can't. You can always control how you look at and deal with what happens to you. You can control your blood pressure, your heart rate, the way you treat people, the commitment you have to your job, how many times you tell your children how much you love them, and a multitude of other things. You always have some control.

Abandon the energy you are throwing at uncontrollable events. It's a waste of time. Salute the reality of change and the fact that you can't control everything in your life. Get on with life by separating the controllable and uncontrollable events in your life, and invest your psychological energies in determining how you will deal with life's detours and opportunities.

We either choose to create the quality of each day or accept a life sentence of wallowing in tension, anger, stress, and discouragement. Refusing to make careful choices when change is all around you allows the events to shape and control your life. Unfortunately, you'll end up emotionally and physically exhausted.

Do you want to change the impact change has on your life? Then change the way you respond to it. As Jungian analyst and philosopher James Hillman has said: "Insanity is doing the same thing over and over again and expecting different results."[3]

> All of life is a series of choices, and what you choose to give life today will determine what life will give you tomorrow.
>
> Zig Ziglar[4]

Chapter 46

CREATE A CHOICE CREDO

There is a better way to live. Choice! The key is choice. You
have options. You need not spend your life wallowing in failure,
ignorance, grief, poverty, shame, and self-pity. But, hold on!
If this is true, then why have so many among us apparently
elected to live in that manner? The answer is obvious. Those
who live in unhappy failure have never exercised their options
for a better way of life because they have never been aware that
they had any choices!

Og Mandino[1]

I LIKE LIFE-ENHANCING PRINCIPLES THAT ARE simple to understand. Og Mandino's observation falls into that category. He
identified a better way to live with just one word. Choice!

I've decided there are three basic things I need to remember
about life:

1. I cannot always control everything that happens to me.
Sometimes I can. Sometimes I can't.

2. I can always control how I respond to any situation. The
attitudes, reactions, and perspectives I experience are my personal
choice.

3. Therefore, I always have some degree of control over my life. Although the circumstances are often uncontrollable, I alone decide how I will respond.

This comprehensive approach has compelled me to create a "choice credo" for my life. It is a self empowering way to remind me of the power I have to make choices and take action. This credo has allowed me to determine my level of dissatisfaction or satisfaction, frustration or contentment, happiness or grief. When I waver from my commitment, a warning light goes off. I feel out of control and a sense of powerlessness sets in.

C.S. Lewis said:

> Every time you make a choice you are turning the control part of you, the part that chooses, into something a little different from what it was before. And taking your life as a whole, with all your innumerable choices, you are slowly turning this control thing either into a heavenly creature or into a hellish one.[2]

Here is the personal credo of choice that helps to turn my relationships, life and career into a "heavenly creature."

CHOICE CREDO

I choose to be excited and enthusiastic about every minute of every day.

I choose to be energetic, productive, and sensitive to how I use my time by carefully determining my priorities.

I choose to apply my energies on solutions, answers, and options rather than becoming engulfed in problems.

I choose to positively affect the lives of people through nurturing, support, and encouragement.

I choose to control my attitude and strive to see the bright side.

I choose to develop the qualities and characteristics that will bring achievement, successful results, and personal fulfillment.

I choose to give every task my best effort and unrestricted energy.

I choose to carefully consider my response to difficult, critical, and controlling people.

I choose to be a caring, loving husband and father, determined to help my family live life to the fullest.

I choose to involve my self in activities that strengthen me physically, mentally, emotionally, and spiritually.

I certainly don't mean to imply I've mastered or perfected my "choice credo." Unfortunately not. It's a daily challenge to live up to the standards expressed. By striving to accept responsibility for my life choices, actions, and attitudes, I'm giving myself permission to determine the quality of my life. When I make wise decisions, I reap positive results. When I choose to become a victim of past experiences, present circumstances or other people, the hope for a better life is deflated.

Don't become a victim of yourself. Determine what is working in your life and what isn't. Is what you're doing today advancing you toward what you want to be tomorrow? Don't go through the day with your fingers crossed saying, "I hope things get better soon." Make choices based upon your values, rather than circumstances or feelings. Do what is right regardless of how you feel. The feelings will follow.

Arnold J. Toynbee said, "As human beings, we are endowed with freedom of choice, and we cannot shuffle off our responsibility upon the shoulders of God or nature. We must shoulder it ourselves. It is up to us."[3] Choose to become all you can be by committing yourself to your own "choice credo."

> In the long run, we shape our lives and we shape ourselves. The process never ends until we die. And the choices we make are ultimately our own responsibility.
>
> Eleanor Roosevelt[4]

Chapter 47

Insist on Internal Accountability

My philosophy is that not only are you responsible for your life,
but doing the best at this moment puts you in the best place for
the next moment.

Oprah Winfrey[1]

THE ABILITY TO ENJOY THE future rests with us and not a
dependence on other people to get us through. Accountability
becomes a reality when you finally realize that no one is
coming to the rescue. The starting point of personal accountability
is for you to accept complete responsibility for who you are and for
everything that you become.

Here's a hint to jump-start your life. *Realize that no one is coming
to your rescue.* The degree to which you effectively deal with change
is in direct proportion to the degree you feel you are in control of
your life.

Victims produce self-imposed stress. They are preoccupied with
the past and uncontrollable experiences filling their life with should-
haves, could-haves, and would-haves. Victims go through the day

with their fingers crossed, hoping things will get better. But they are convinced nothing they do will change their condition. Victims see themselves controlled by external circumstances. They put other people in charge of their moods. It's a no-win lifestyle created by a loser mind set.

Your attitude toward personal accountability is one of the most important statements you make about the kind of person you are and the degree of control you exhibit in your life. Taking responsibility for future results sows the seeds of positive emotions. It's great to have people around you to encourage, support, express appreciation, and offer assistance. Becoming dependent on others breeds disappointment and turns change into a threat. The old saying, "If it is to be, it is up to me" serves us well here.

Competency, security, job satisfaction, personal fulfillment, and emotional health are an inside job. Nobody has been assigned to your case to insure your successful journey through present and future passages. "I am responsible." Say it to yourself. Repeat it frequently. Accept it as a reality and mandatory course of study and mastery throughout the rest of your life.

No doubt about it; change is a learning experience. As Mark Twain observed, "A man who holds a cat by the tail learns something he can learn in no other way."[2] You're right, Mr. Twain, and change also forces us to look at life's changing menu with maturing perspective.

Courageously face life with its uncertainties. There is a world full of opportunities waiting to be seized. Shedding old skin may involve pain, tears, sweat, and failure; but it clears your vision and motivates you to capture your dreams, build a better you, and enjoy this thing called life.

> Live in such a way that you would not be ashamed to sell your parrot to the town gossip.
>
> Will Rogers[3]

NOTES

SECTION 1: EMBRACE CHANGE

Chapter 1: Enjoy Life in Times of Change

1. John F. Kennedy, Citation unknown.
2. Source unknown.
3. U.S. Census Bureau, http://www.census.gov/.
4. Dr. Joyce Brothers, Citation unknown.
5. Bob Moawad, quoted on *randomquotes.org*, http://randomquotes. org/quote/15743-you-cant-leave-footprints-in-the-sands-of-time-if.html.
6. Gwendolyn Brooks, quoted on *viptonline.com*, http://viptonline. com/quotes.aspx.

Chapter 2: Give of Yourself

1. Alan Loy McGinnis, quoted on *thinkinexist.com*, http://thinkexist. com/quotation/there_is_no_more_noble_occupation_in_the_ world/160486.html.
2. Source unknown.
3. *An Officer and a Gentleman*, written by Douglas Day Stewart and directed by Taylor Hackford, 124 minutes, Capitol Equipment Leasing and Lorimar Film Entertainment, 1982, videocassette.
4. Ben Sweetland, quoted on *thinkexist.com*, http://thinkexist.com/ quotation/we_cannot_hold_a_torch_to_light_another-s_path/12870.html.

Chapter 3: Commit Yourself to a Change-Ready Lifestyle

1. Abbie Hoffman, quoted in *Fate's Redemption* by Keith Lee Johnson (New York: Strebor Books, 2001), i.

2. Mark Twain, *The Adventures of Huckleberry Finn*, (New York, Charles L. Webster and Company, 1885), 14.

3. Dean Rusk, quoted in *TIME*, "The Quiet Man," http://www.time.com/time/magazine/article/0,9171,898079-1,00.html.

4. Faith Popcorn, *The Popcorn Report*, Citation unknown.

5. Rosabeth Moss Kanter, *The Change Masters: Corporate Entrepreneurs at Work* (New York: Free Press, 1985), 65.

6. Eddy Ketchursid, Citation unknown.

7. Harold Wilson, quoted on *WorldofQuotes.com*, http://www.worldofquotes.com/author/Harold-Wilson/1/index.html.

Section 2: Make the Best of It
Chapter 4: Don't Beat Yourself Up

1. Hugh White, quoted on *wisequotes.net*, http://www.wisequotes.net/quote/18922-when-you-make-a-mistake-dont-look-back-at-it-lon.html.

2. Peanuts Cartoon, Citation unknown.

3. Sophia Loren, Citation unknown.

4. Paul "Bear" Bryant, quoted on *"quote" BANK*, http://www.coachqte.com/bryant.html.

5. Napoleon Hill, *The Law of Success Complete*, (Thousand Oaks, CA: BN Publishing, 2008).

6. "Intel Hit by Pentium III Flaw," *BBC News*, http://news.bbc.co.uk/1/hi/business/744648.stm.

7. Winston Churchill, *The Churchill War Papers: The Ever-Widening War*, (New York: W. W. Norton & Company, 2001), 1086.

8. Dale Carnegie, quoted on *brainyquote.com*, http://www.brainyquote.com/quotes/authors/d/dale_carnegie.html.

9. Humorous story, Source unknown.

10. Benjamin Franklin, quoted on *quotationsbook.com*, http://quotationsbook.com/author/2619/page=12/.

11. Anonymous, quoted on *famousquotesandauthors.com*, http://www.famousquotesandauthors.com/topics/mistakes_and_blunders_quotes.html.

12. Humorous story, Source unknown.

13. Pearl Buck, quoted on *The Quotations Page*, http://www.quotationspage.com/quote/3104.html.

14. Jerry Jenkins, quoted in *The Power of Thinking Big* by John C. Maxwell (Colorado Springs, CO: David C. Cook, 2001), 108.

Chapter 5: Life Can Be a Bummer

1. Charles Lindbergh, quoted on *BlogNet*, http://successblognet.com/successful-quotes-famous-people/.

2. M. Scott Peck, *The Road Less Traveled: A New Psychology of Love, Traditional Values and Spiritual Growth* (New York: Touchstone, 2003).

3. Walt Disney, quoted on *goodreads*, http://www.goodreads.com/quotes/show/27106.

4. "John Grisham," *Academy of Achievement*, http://www.achievement.org/autodoc/page/gri0bio-1.

5. Harry Emerson Fosdick, Citation unknown.

6. Jane Pauley, Citation unknown.

7. Lou Holtz, quoted on *Quotations Book*, http://quotationsbook.com/quote/1041/.

8. New York Times, "Question Of the Week; Who Was The Best Performer Of 1988?", http://query.nytimes.com/gst/fullpage.html?res=9C0CE3DE1326E733BC4953DFBF6E958A.

9. William Arthur Ward, quoted on *thinkexist.com*, http://thinkexist.com/quotation/adversity_causes_some_men_to_break-others_to/227361.html.

10. "Franklin D. Roosevelt," *The White House*, http://www.whitehouse.gov/about/presidents/franklindroosevelt/.

11. Terry Egan, *The Good Guys of Baseball* (New York: Aladdin, 2000), 70-79.

12. Margaret Paul, *Today's Woman*, http://www.todays-woman.net/article1854.html.

13. Napoleon Hill, quoted on *MotivateUs.com*, http://www.motivateus.com/cust-11.htm.

14. Robert Schuller, Citation unknown.

15. "Lee Iacocca," *Bizography: the business biography site*, http://www.bizography.org/biographies/lee-iacocca.html.

16. "Vanessa Williams," *IBDb*, http://www.imdb.com/name/nm0001853/bio.

17. Samuel Johnson, quoted in *thinkexist.com*, http://thinkexist.com/quotation/life_affords_no_higher_pleasure_than_that_of/8313.html.

18. B.C. Forbes, quoted on *Brainy Quote*, http://www.brainyquote.com/quotes/quotes/b/bcforbes126457.html.

19. Humorist, Source unknown.

20. Malcolm Forbes, quoted on *Said What?*, http://www.saidwhat.co.uk/quotes/favourite/malcolm_forbes/when_things_are_bad_we_take_8966.

21. William James, quoted on *Famous Quotes & Authors*, http://www.famousquotesandauthors.com/authors/william_james_quotes.html.

22. Henry Ward Beecher, quoted on *UBR, Inc.*, http://www.people.ubr.com/historical-figures/by-first-name/h/henry-ward-beecher/henry-ward-beecher-quotes.aspx.

23. Stedham Graham, Source unknown.

24. Norman Vincent Peale, *Enthusiasm Makes the Difference* (New York: Fireside, 2003), 178.

25. Charles R. Woodson, Citation unknown.

Chapter 6: Escape the Bottom of the Can

1. Les Brown, quoted on *thinkexist.com*, http://thinkexist.com/quotation/we_must_look_for_ways_to_be_an_active_force_in/344557.html.

2. Mohandas Gandhi, quoted on *The Quote Blog*, http://www.thequoteblog.com/mahatma-gandhi-on-freedom/.

3. Benjamin Elijah Mays, quoted on *Social Science Research Network*, http://papers.ssrn.com/sol3/papers.cfm?abstract_id=910387.

4. Kurt D. Bruner, Citation unknown.

Chapter 7: Be Better than Average

1. William Faulkner, quoted on *goodreads*, http://www.goodreads.com/quotes/show/21210.

2. Edmund Gaudet, quoted on *Are You Average?*, http://www.theexaminer.org/volume8/number1/average.htm.

3. Jane Wagner, *The Search for Signs of Intelligent Life in the Universe* (Harper Paperbacks, 1991) 25-26.

4. Phillips Brooks, *Daily Thoughts from Phillips Brooks* (Baltimore, MD: R.H. Woodward & Co., 1893), 85.

5. Kathleen Norris, quoted on *Mediocrity Quotes*, http://www.wisdomquotes.com/cat_mediocrity.html.

Section 3: Remember, It Could Be Worse

Chapter 8: Learn to Expect (and Enjoy) the Unexpected

1. Eleanor Roosevelt, quoted on *Brainy Quote*, http://www.brainyquote. com/quotes/quotes/e/eleanorroo384413.html.

2. Charles M. Schulz, *Peanuts*, http://comics.com/peanuts.

3. Anonymous, Source unknown.

4. Kathleen Norris, quoted on *The Literature Network*, http://www. online-literature.com/kathleen-norris/.

5. Madeleine L'Engle, quoted on *SOUL N PEACE.com*, http://www. soulnpeace.com/related/motivational-quotes/quotes-8.html.

6. George Gissing, quoted on *The Private Papers of Henry Ryecroft*, www.litquotes.com.

7. Gregory Bateson, quoted on *Famous Quotes & Authors*, http://www. famousquotesandauthors.com/authors/gregory_bateson_quotes.html.

8. Rick Pitino, *Success Is a Choice: Ten Steps to Overachieving in Business and Life* (New York: Broadway, 1998), 196.

Chapter 9: Hang on Through Turbulent Times

1. Paraphrase of M. Scott Peck, *The Road Less Traveled: A New Psychology of Love, Traditional Values and Spiritual Growth* (New York: Touchstone, 2003), 15.

2. Mafu, quoted in *Leadership by Encouragement* by Don Dinkmeyer (Boca Raton, FL: CRC Press, 1996), 214.

3. Andy Duncan, *Alabama Curiosities*, (Guilford, CT: Globe Pequot, 2005), 86–87.

4. Craig Brian Larson, *Illustrations for Preaching and Teaching from Leadership Journal* (Grand Rapids, MI: Baker Book House, 1993), 114.

5. Malcolm Forbes, quoted by Christy Schmidt in "Overcoming Obstacles to Problem Solving, Or: What to Do When Finding the Solution to a Problem Becomes a Problem," *The Beacon*, http://www.miller-schmidt.com/beacon/2005novdec.html.

Chapter 10: Recognize the Value of Catfish

1. Eleanor Roosevelt, quoted on *Brainy Quote*, http://www.brainyquote. com/quotes/authors/e/eleanor_roosevelt.html.

2. Luke 4:1-13, *Holy Bible, New International Version*, (International Bible Society, 1984).

3. William Penn, quoted on *The Quotations Page*, http://www. quotationspage.com/quote/8559.html.

4. Charles Swindoll, quoted by James S. Hewett in *Illustrations Unlimited* (Wheaton: Tyndale House Publishers, Inc, 1988), 14.

5. John 8:58, *Holy Bible, New International Version*, (International Bible Society, 1984).

6. Eleanor Roosevelt, *You Learn By Living* (New York: Harper, 1960), 29-30.

7. Annette Funicello, *A Dream Is a Wish Your Heart Makes* (New York: Little, Brown and Company, 1995).

Chapter 11: Break Through the Brick Wall of Adversity

1. Charles Lindbergh, quoted on *BlogNet*, http://successblognet.com/ successful-quotes-famous-people/.

2. "Joni Eareckson Tada," *historyswomen.com*, http://www. historyswomen.com/historyinthemaking/joni.html.

3. Helen Keller, quoted on *Thinkexist.com*, http://thinkexist.com/ quotation/literature_is_my_utopia-here_i_am_not/209203.html.

4. Michael LeBoeuf, quoted on *Self Help Daily*, http://www. selfhelpdaily.com/SelfHelpQuotes/trouble.html.

5. Steve Kemp, Citation unknown.

6. Warren Wiersbe, Citation unknown.

7. Norman Vincent Peale, *Enthusiasm Makes the Difference* (New York: Fireside, 2003), 178.

8. James Brady, quoted on *Famous Quotes & Authors*, http://www. famousquotesandauthors.com/authors/james_brady_quotes.html.

SECTION 4: DE-STRESS YOUR STRESS

Chapter 12: How to Keep from Being Wired and Tired

1. Charles Swindoll, Citation unknown.

2. Success magazine, quoted on *Spouses Who Sell Houses.ca*, http://spouseswhosellhouses.ca/allquotes. cfm?PageNum_rsThoughts=11&CFNoCache=TRUE.

3. Michael LeBoeuf, quoted on *SuccessGroove*, http://successgroove. com/success-quotes/overistimating-stress.html.

4. "Worry," *Merriam Webster Online*, http://www.merriam-webster. com/dictionary/worry.

5. Ralph Waldo Emerson, quoted on *Start Winning EveryDay*, http://www.startwinningeveryday.com/quotes.htm.

6. John E. Newman, *How to Stay Cool, Calm & Collected When the Pressure's On* (New York: MJF Books, 2002), 36.

Chapter 13: A Primer on Mastering Stress

1. Hans Selye, Citation unknown.

2. Hans Selye, Citation unknown.

3. Paul Rosch, quoted by the *American Institute of Stress*, http://www.stress.org/.

4. Candice Bergen, Citation unknown.

Chapter 14: Survival of the Stressed

1. Tug McGraw, quoted on *Famous Quotes & Authors*, http://www.famousquotesandauthors.com/authors/tug_mcgraw_quotes.html.

2. Report by *CNN*, http://www.cnn.com/.

3. Report by *Associated Press*, http://www.ap.org/.

4. Study by *National Mental Health Association*, http://www.nmha.org/.

5. Report by *Business Week*, http://www.businessweek.com/.

6. Facts gathered by *Wellness First Family Chiropractic*, http://www.wellnessfirst.ca/Articles/E5-Medical%20Facts.doc.

7. Story, Source unknown.

8. Lily Tomlin, quoted by *Firm Counsel*, http://www.firmcounsel.co.uk/?p=48.

9. "Concorde," http://www.concordesst.com/.

10. Anthony Robbins, *Awaken the Giant Within* (Mankato, MN: Free Press, 1992), 114.

11. Earle Wilson, quoted in "Business Communication and Executive Effectiveness" on *Scribd*, http://www.scribd.com/doc/7076977/SCDL-PGDBA-Finance-Sem-1-Business-Communication-Executive-Effectiveness.

12. Dr. Paul Rosch, quoted in "Get a Grip on Job Stress," by Denise Kersten, *USATODAY.COM*, November 12, 2002, http://www.usatoday.com/money/jobcenter/workplace/stressmanagement/2002-11-12-job-stress_x.htm.

13. Gerald Loren Fishkin, http://drgeraldfishkin.com/.

14. George Salvadore Stevenson, *How to Deal with Your Tensions* (Alexandria, VA: National Association for Mental Health, 1957).

15. 1 Peter 5:7, *Holy Bible, New International Version,* (International Bible Society, 1984).

16. Corrie Ten Boom, quoted on *goodreads,* http://www.goodreads.com/author/quotes/102203.Corrie_Ten_Boom.

17. Hans Selye, quoted by Gloria M. Davenport in *Working with Toxic Older Adults: A Guide to Coping with Difficult Elders* (New York: Springer Publishing Company, 2006), 245.

18. Reverend Louis Lotz, Source unknown.

Chapter 15: Learn the Lessons of Failure

1. Harvey Mackay, Citation unknown.

2. Ty Boyd, Citation unknown.

3. Charles M. Schulz, *Peanuts,* http://comics.com/peanuts.

4. "Orville Redenbacher Biography," *Biography.com,* http://www.biography.com/search/article.do?id=248523.

5. "Michael Jeffrey Jordan," *NBA Encyclopedia,* http://www.nba.com/history/players/jordan_bio.html.

6. "'NIGROSIN,' CANCER ANTIDOTE; Name Chosen by Prof. Ehrlich—100 Per Cent. of Mice Cured." *The New York Times,* February 9, 1912, http://query.nytimes.com/gst/abstract.html?res=9F01EFD7123AE633A2575AC0A9649C946396D6CF.

7. "Supremes," *Wikipedia.org,* http://en.wikipedia.org/wiki/The_Supremes.

8. Winston Churchill, quoted on *brainyquote.com,* http://www.brainyquote.com/quotes/quotes/w/winstonchu108950.html

9. Edwin Louis Cole, Citation unknown.

10. Tom Hopkins, quoted on *thinkexist.com,* http://thinkexist.com/quotation/i_am_not_judged_by_the_number_of_times_i_fail-but/151243.html

Section 5: Live to Learn and Learn to Live

Chapter 16: No Coasting Allowed

1. Charles R. Swindoll, *Three Steps Forward, Two Steps Back* (Nashville, TN: Thomas Nelson, 1998), 2.

2. Cullen Hightower, quoted on *Total Health: Caring for the Whole Person,* http://www.totalhealth.bz/health-quotes-miscellaneous.htm.

3. Tom Clancy, quoted on *thinkexist.com,* http://thinkexist.com/quotes/tom_clancy/.

Chapter 17: Get Curious

1. Eugene S. Wilson, quoted on *Said What?*, http://www.saidwhat.co.uk/quotes/famous/eugene_wilson/only_the_curious_will_learn_and_31809.

2. William A. Ward, quoted on *thinkexist.com*, http://thinkexist.com/quotation/curiosity_is_the_wick_in_the_candle_of_learning/15188.html.

3. Portia Nelson, *There's a Hole in My Sidewalk* (New York, NY: Simon and Schuster, 1993) 2–3.

4. Archibald MacLeish, quoted on *thinkexist.com*, http://thinkexist.com/quotation/there_is_only_one_thing_more_painful_than/221237.html.

5. Yogi Berra, quoted on *thinkexist.com*, http://thinkexist.com/quotation/you_can_observe_a_lot_just_by_watching/150214.html.

6. Max DePree, quoted on *Gifted Leaders LLC*, http://www.giftedleaders.com/quotes.htm.

Chapter 18: How Informed Are You?

1. Malcolm S. Forbes, quoted on *brainyquote.com*, http://www.brainyquote.com/quotes/authors/m/malcolm_forbes.html.

2. Professor Herb Dordick, quoted on *Tina Lewis Rowe: a Journal of Information, Inspiration and Insight*, http://tinalewisrowe.com/2008/03/.

3. Story about Bill McGowan, *Success Magazine*, Source unknown.

4. Story about Charlie Steinmetz, Source unknown.

5. Robert Heller, *Super Manager* (New York: McGraw Hill, 1987).

6. Johann Wolfgang von Goethe, quoted on *thinkexist.com*, http://thinkexist.com/quotation/all_the_knowledge_i_possess_everyone_else_can/210055.html.

7. Napoleon Hill, *Think and Grow Rich* (Lafayette, LA: Filiquarian Publishing, LLC, 2005), 77.

8. Theodore Roosevelt, Citation unknown.

9. "An Account of the Life of John Wesley," from expanded *Foxe's Book of Martyrs*, edited by William Byron Forbush, http://gbgm-umc.org/UMW/Wesley/foxwesley.stm.

10. Abraham Lincoln, quoted by Max D. Isaacson in *How to Conquer the Fear of Public Speaking and Other Coronary Threats* (Rockville Centre, NY: Farnsworth Publishing, Co., 1964) 21.

11. Peter Senge, *The Fifth Discipline* (New York: Random House, Inc., 2006).

Chapter 19: Ignite Your Innovative Spirit

1. William Arthur Ward, quoted by F. David Webster and Tolulope A. Adeleye, *Stay Sane Through Change* (Martinsburg, WV: Holy Fire Publishing, 2005) 187.

2. "Jerome H. Lemelson," *The Lemelson Foundation*, http://www. lemelson.org/about/bio_jerry.php.

3. "Dick Fosbury," *Wikipedia: The Free Encyclopedia*, http:// en.wikipedia.org/wiki/Dick_Fosbury.

4. Sid Caesar, quoted on *brainyquote.com*, http://www.brainyquote. com/quotes/quotes/s/sidcaesar176193.html.

Section 6: Rethink What You Think

Chapter 20: Accentuate the Positive

1. Walt Whitman, quoted on *thinkexist.com*, http://thinkexist.com/ quotation/keep_your_face_always_toward_the_sunshine-and/254859. html.

2. "Drosera-Sundews," *Botanique: Carnivorous and Unusual Plants*, http://www.pitcherplant.com/drosera.html#cat_dbin.

3. Dan Millman, *Way of the Peaceful Warrior* (Tiburon, CA: H. J. Kramer, Inc., 2006), 50.

4. Lydia H. Sigourney, quoted by Tryon Edwards, *A Dictionary of Thoughts* (Detroit, MI: F. B. Dickerson Company, 1908), 501.

Chapter 21: Break the Chains

1. Napoleon Bonaparte, quoted on *thinkexist.com*, http://thinkexist. com/quotation/impossible_is_a_word_to_be_found_only_in_the/216934. html.

2. "Ramananda" at University of Minnesota, Source unknown.

3. Charles F. Kettering, quoted on *QuotationsBook*, http:// quotationsbook.com/quote/32096/.

4. "Susie Maroney," *the Insider*, http://www.theinsider.com/ celebrities/Susie_Maroney.

5. Doug Larson, quoted on *The Quotations Page*, http://www. quotationspage.com/quote/37635.html.

6. General Leslie Groves, quoted in "Success Quotations," by *The Cole Family Multi-Media WebPage*, http://www.steveandeileencole.com/ success_hide.htm.

Chapter 22: Don't Poison the Environment

1. Charles Swindoll, Citation unknown.

2. "Unknown article," *Psychology Today*, Citation unknown.

3. Robert Kennedy, quoted on *thinkexist.com*, http://thinkexist.com/ quotation/one-fifth_of_the_people_are_against_everything/224051.html.

4. Chris Evert, quoted by Keith Johnson, *The Confidence Makeover* (Shippensburg, PA: Destiny Image Publishers, Inc., 2006), 86.

Chapter 23: Look for the Blue Sky

1. William Arthur Ward, quoted on *thinkexist.com*, http://thinkexist. com/quotation/the_pessimist_complains_about_the_wind-the/227505. html.

2. Martin Seligman, *Learned Optimism* (NY: Free Press, 1998).

3. *Forrest Gump*, directed by Robert Zemeckis, 142 minutes, Paramount Pictures, 1994, DVD.

4. Harry Truman, quoted on *brainyquote.com*, http://www.brainyquote. com/quotes/quotes/h/harrystru161812.html.

5. George Will, quoted on *The Quotations Page*, http://www. quotationspage.com/quote/38892.html.

6. Pogo cartoon, quoted by Bob Fisher, Bethel Thomas, and Bo Thomas, *Real Dream Teams* (Boca Raton, FL: CRC Press LLC, 1996), 52.

7. Rene Descartes, quoted on *Said What? Quotations*, http://www.saidwhat.co.uk/quotes/famous/rene_descartes/ an_optimist_may_see_a_light_1703.

Section 7: Stay Balanced

Chapter 24: Keep Life's Irritations in Perspective

1. Victor Frankl, quoted on *thinkexist.com*, http://thinkexist.com/ search/searchquotation.asp?search=Man%92s+last+freedom+is+his+fre edom+to+choose+how+he+will+react+in+any+given+situation&q=author %3A%22Viktor+Frankl%22.

2. Alfred North Whitehead, quoted on *FamousQuotes.com*, http://www. famousquotes.com/search.php?search=wholly.

Chapter 25: It's Time to Deal with Overload

1. Henry A. Kissinger, quoted on *BrainyQuote*, http://www.brainyquote. com/quotes/quotes/h/henryakis399125.html.

2. CNN poll, *CNN.com*, Citation unknown.

3. Elaine St. James, quoted on *Quotatio: 50,000+ Quotations*, http://www.quotatio.com/j/james-elaine-st-no-one-can-maintain-more-than-three-100139.html.

Chapter 26: Energize Your Abilities and Keep Learning

1. Theodore Roosevelt, Citation unknown.

2. Ken Medema, Citation unknown.

3. Eric Hoffer, quoted on *thinkexist.com*, http://thinkexist.com/quotation/in_a_time_of_drastic_change_it_is_the_learners/10724.html.

4. Winston Churchill, quoted on *QuotationsBook*, http://quotationsbook.com/quote/187/.

5. George Sheehan, quoted on *thinkexist.com*, http://thinkexist.com/quotation/if_you_want_to_win_anything-a_race-yourself-your/175467.html.

Chapter 27: Enjoy the Ride

1. Steven Leacock, quoted on *BrainyQuote*, http://www.brainyquote.com/quotes/quotes/s/stephenlea153182.html.

2. "Nissan is changing the rules for car ads by rolling out entertaining spots using toy characters," *New York Times*, October 24, 1996.

3. Steven Wright, quoted on *BrainyQuote*, http://www.brainyquote.com/quotes/quotes/s/stevenwrig107861.html.

4. Lyndon B. Johnson, Source unknown.

5. Lily Tomlin, quoted on *thinkexist.com*, http://thinkexist.com/quotation/the_trouble_with_the_rat-race_is_that_even_if_you/8038.html.

6. Helen Keller, "Three Days to See," *Atlantic Monthly*, January, 1933.

7. Thornton Wilder, quoted on *Famous Quotes & Authors*, http://www.famousquotesandauthors.com/authors/thornton_wilder_quotes.html.

Section 8: Live Life to the Fullest
Chapter 28: Live in the Now

1. Linda Ellerbee, Citation unknown.

2. Jim Davis, *Garfield*, http://www.garfield.com/.

3. Ellen Glasgow, quoted on *BrainyQuote*, http://www.brainyquote.com/quotes/quotes/e/ellenglasg383452.html.

4. W. Mitchell, Citation unknown.

Chapter 29: Loosen Your Grip

1. Steve Rapson, quoted on *QuotationsBook*, http://quotationsbook. com/quote/8366/.

2. Agatha Christie, quoted on *Famous Quotes & Authors*, http://www. famousquotesandauthors.com/authors/agatha_christie_quotes.ht

Chapter 30: Hold Tight to Your Purpose

1. Mary Wollstonecraft Shelley, quoted on *thinkexist.com*, http:// thinkexist.com/quotation/nothing_contributes_so_much_to_tranquilize_ the/184752.html.

2. Napoleon Hill, Citation unknown.

3. "Mother Teresa," *Nobelprize.org*, http://nobelprize.org/nobel_ prizes/peace/laureates/1979/teresa-bio.html.

4. James Allen, *As a Man Thinketh*, (Rockville, MD: Arc Manor, 2007), 34.

5. Orison Swett Marden, *Pushing to the Front* (Phoenix, AZ: Wilder Publications, 2008), 499.

6. Earl Nightingale, "Earl Nightingale on Winning: The Common Denominator for Success," Nightingale-Conant Corp., 1978, audio cassette.

Chapter 31: Loosen Up! Lighten Up! Live It Up!

1. Mark Twain, quoted on *thinkexist.com*, http://thinkexist.com/ quotation/humor_is_the_great_thing-the_saving_thing-the/215016.html.

2. Roger Ailes, "Lighten Up: Stuffed Shirts Have Short Careers," *Newsweek* (New York), May 1992.

3. Unnamed poll, *Entertainment Weekly*, Citation unknown.

4. Bob Hope, quoted on *thinkexist.com*, http://thinkexist.com/ quotation/i_have_seen_what_a_laugh_can_do-it_can_transform/199718. html.

5. Norman Cousins, Citation unknown.

6. Josh Billings, Citation unknown.

Section 9: Cultivate a Fun Spirit
Chapter 32: Renew the Child in You

1. Michael Pritchard, quoted on *thinkexist.com*, http://thinkexist.com/quotation/we_don-t_stop_laughing_because_we_grow_old-we/186258.html.

2. Alvin Schwartz, quoted in *Laffirmations* by Joel Goodman (Deerfield Beach, FL: HCI, 1995).

3. Benjamin Hoff, *Tao of Pooh*, (New York: Penguin, 1994).

4. Laurence J. Peter and Bill Dana, *The Laughter Prescription* (New York: Ballantine, 1982).

Chapter 33: Listen for Life's Laughable Moments

1. Will Rogers, quoted on *The Quotations Page*, http://www.quotationspage.com/quote/134.html.

2. Linda Ellerbee, quoted in "Surviving Breast Cancer," *McCall's Magazine*, October, 1993.

3. Linda Ellerbee, quoted on *thinkexist.com*, http://thinkexist.com/quotes/linda_ellerbee/.

4. Anne Wilson Schaef, quoted on *Famous Quotes & Authors*, http://www.famousquotesandauthors.com/authors/anne_wilson_schaef_quotes.html.

Chapter 34: Think Funny

1. H. Jackson Brown, *Life's Little Treasure Book Series*, (Nashville, TN: Thomas Nelson, 1994).

2. Ronald Reagan, quoted on *thinkexist.com*, http://thinkexist.com/quotation/i_hope_you-re_all_republicans--to_surgeons_as_he/338217.html.

3. Story about President and Mrs. Reagan, Source unknown.

4. James Russell Lowell, quoted by Malford W. Thewlis in "Geriatrics," *Medical Review of Reviews* Vol. XXIV, January-December, 1918, 95-97.

5. Story about golfer, told on *Mr. Golf Etiquette's Really Good Golf Jokes*, http://www.mrgolf.com/jokes.html.

6. Garrison Keillor, quoted on *goodreads*, http://www.goodreads.com/author/quotes/2014.Garrison_Keillor.

Chapter 35: Willing to Laugh at Yourself

1. Charles Schultz, quoted on *BrainyQuote*, http://www.brainyquote.com/quotes/quotes/c/charlesms121692.html.

2. Dr. John Maxwell, Citation unknown.

3. Joel Goodman, quoted by W. Bradford Swift in "Humor Experts Jazz up the Workplace." *HR Magazine*, March 1994, http://findarticles.com/p/articles/mi_m3495/is_n3_v39/ai_15379395/.

4. G. K. Chesterton, Source unknown.

5. Bald jokes, citations unknown.

6. John Powell, quoted on *thinkexist.com*, http://thinkexist.com/quotation/blessed_is_he_who_has_learned_to_laugh_at_himself/156044.html.

7. Ethel Barrymore, quoted on *QuotationsBook*, http://quotationsbook.com/quote/22456/.

8. Art Gliner, quoted on *sarahtory.com*, http://www.sarahtory.com/quotes.html.

SECTION 10: SEEK NEW HORIZONS

Chapter 36: Notice Opportunities

1. Rita Cooledge, quoted on *BrainyQuote*, http://www.brainyquote.com/quotes/quotes/r/ritacoolid335198.html.

2. Jack Welch, "Leadership Secret 1: Harness the Power of Change," from *The Files of Jack Welch*, Citation unknown.

3. Plutarch, quoted by Arthur Richard Shilleto in *Plutarch's Morals* (London: George Bell & Sons, 1888), 293.

4. "Home Shopping Network," *Wikipedia: The Free Encyclopedia*, http://en.wikipedia.org/wiki/Home_Shopping_Network.

5. Kevin Kelly, "The Nine Laws of God," *Whole Earth Catalog*, Spring, 1994, http://wholeearth.com/issue/1330/article/338/the.nine.laws.of.god.

6. Alexander Graham Bell, quoted on *thinkexist.com*, http://thinkexist.com/quotation/when_one_door_closes-another_opens-but_we_often/12671.html.

7. Bernie Siegel, Citation unknown.

Chapter 37: Move Boldly into the Unknown

1. David Viscott, *Risking* (New York: Pocket, 1990).

2. Edward de Bono and Robert Heller, "Entrepreneurs: Nine qualities of entrepreneurship," *Thinking Managers*, http://www.thinkingmanagers.com/management/entrepreneurs.php.

3. "Sony's Legend Stepping Down," *USA Today*, Citation unknown.

4. Louis L'Amour, quoted on "The Eternal Frontier" worksheet, http://soe.ucdavis.edu/ss0809/CraggsM/Fall%2008%20Unit/Handouts/EternalFrontierWorksheet.pdf.

5. "Story," quoted on *The Good Life: Reflections on the Eternal Quest for The Good Life*, November, 2005.

6. Virgil Thomson, quoted on *BrainyQuote*, http://www.brainyquote.com/quotes/quotes/v/virgilthom163833.html.

7. Dr. Susie Jeffries, Source unknown.

8. Bruce Barton, quoted on *thinkexist.com*, http://thinkexist.com/quotation/nothing_splendid_has_ever_been_achieved_except_by/167545.html.

9. Toni Flores, quoted on *Quote Monster*, http://www.sujal.net/quotes/viewall.php3?start_value=40&range=20&collection_id=.

10. Ray Bradbury, quoted on *QuotationsBook*, http://quotationsbook.com/quote/34663/.

Chapter 38: The Fun Is in the Challenge

1. Paul Harvey, quoted by Mary Bauer, "How Do Successful People Get Successful—They Follow These Ten Rules," *EzineArticles.com*, March, 2007, http://ezinearticles.com/?How-Do-Successful-People-Get-Successful-They-Follow-These-10-Rules&id=488972.

2. "Tom Monaghan," *Wikipedia: the Free Encyclopedia*, http://en.wikipedia.org/wiki/Tom_Monaghan.

3. Story about Tom Monaghan and Ray Kroc, Source unknown.

4. Joseph Addison, quoted on *The Quotations Page*, http://www.quotationspage.com/quote/2961.html.

Chapter 39: Too Fat to Fly

1. Harold Mayfield, quoted by Don Soderquist, *The Wal-Mart Way: The Inside Story of the Success of the World's Largest Company*, (Nashville, TN: Thomas Nelson, 2005), 140.

2. Story told by Soren Kierkegaard, Citation unknown.

3. Thomas Edison, quoted on *The Quotations Page*, http://www. quotationspage.com/quote/34594.html.

4. Reggie Leach, quoted on *The Quotations Page*, http://www. quotationspage.com/quote/1963.html.

SECTION 11: GO FOR IT!

Chapter 40: Resist Complacency

1. J. Willard Marriot Sr., Citation unknown.

2. Pablo Casals, quoted by Myles Munroe in *Myles Munroe Devotional & Journal* (Shippensburg, PA: Destiny Image, 2007), Week 37, Day 1.

3. Joe Paterno, quoted on *thinkexist.com*, http://thinkexist.com/ quotation/the-minute-you-think-you-ve-got-it-made-disaster/364173. html.

4. Thomas Edison, quoted on *BrainyQuote*, http://www.brainyquote. com/quotes/quotes/t/thomasaed149052.html.

5. Barbara Walters, quoted on *QuotationsBook*, http://quotationsbook. com/quote/37835/.

6. Thomas Huxley, quoted on *Entrepreneur*, http://www.entrepreneur. com/tradejournals/article/53376337.html.

Chapter 41: Exercise Your Mind

1. William Danforth, quoted on *CreatingMinds.org*, http:// creatingminds.org/quotes/challenge.htm.

2. Campbell's Chunky Soup story, Citation unknown.

3. "Buckminster Fuller," *Wikipedia: The Free Encyclopedia*, http:// en.wikipedia.org/wiki/Buckminster_Fuller.

4. R. Buckminster Fuller, quoted on *Heroes for a Better World*, http:// www.betterworld.net/heroes/pages-f/fuller-buckminster-quotes.htm.

5. "James Murray Spangler," http://spanglers.info/james.htm.

6. USA Today article, Citation unknown.

7. "Pablo Picasso," *Wikipedia: The Free Encylopedia*, http:// en.wikipedia.org/wiki/Pablo_Picasso.

8. Pablo Picasso, quoted on *BrainyQuote*, http://www.brainyquote. com/quotes/quotes/p/pablopicas108723.html.

9. Anand Shah, *Friday Reflections* (BookSurge Publishing, 2007), 13-14.

10. Everett M. Rogers, *Diffusion of Innovations* (Mankato, MN: Free Press, 2003).

11. Albert Einstein, quoted on *thinkexist.com*, http://thinkexist.com/quotation/to_raise_new_questions-new_possibilities-to/222360.html.

12. "History of the Board Game Monopoly," *Monopoly Board*, http://monopolyboard.net/history.

13. Story about Hookless Fastener Company, Source unknown.

14. "Company Overview," *Velcro*, http://www.velcro.com/index.php?page=who-is-velcro-r.

15. Dr. Michael LeBoeuf, Citation unknown.

16. Pablo Picasso, quoted on *thinkexist.com*, http://thinkexist.com/quotation/some_painters_transform_the_sun_into_a_yellow/143236.html.

Chapter 42: What's Your Secret, Mr. Smith?

1. Harold Kushner, quoted by Wes Hanson in *The Power of Character: Prominent Americans Talk about Life, Family, Work, Values and More* (Bloomington, IN: Josephson Institute & Unlimited Publishing LLC, 2004), 11.

2. *Today Show*, Citation unknown.

3. Richard Gaylord Briley, Citation unknown.

4. Supreme Court Justice Oliver Wendell Holmes, Citation unknown.

5. George Bernard Shaw, "Man and Superman: a Comedy and a Philosophy" in *Epistle Dedicatory to Arthur Bingham Walkley*, Citation unknown.

6. George Washington Carver, quoted in "George Washington Carver: Chemist, Teacher, Symbol," *National Historic Chemical Landmarks*, http://acswebcontent.acs.org/landmarks/landmarks/carver/carver.html.

Chapter 43: Success Is Just Around the Corner

1. Harriet Beecher Stowe, quoted on *thinkexist.com*, http://thinkexist.com/quotes/harriet_beecher_stowe/.

2. Quote regarding Walter Payton, Citation unknown.

3. Rush Limbaugh, quoted by John C. Maxwell in *Talent is Never Enough Workbook* (Nashville, TN: Thomas Nelson, 2007), 87.

4. "Malcolm Forbes," *Wikipedia: The Free Encyclopedia*, http://en.wikipedia.org/wiki/Malcolm_Forbes.

5. "Walt Disney," *Wikipedia: The Free Encyclopedia*, http://en.wikipedia.org/wiki/Walt_Disney.

6. Ella Fitzgerald, quoted on *thinkexist.com*, http://thinkexist.com/quotation/just_don-t_give_up_on_trying_to_do_what_you/8845.html.

7. G. Kingsley Ward, *Mark My Words: Letters of a Businessman to His Son* (New York: Simon & Schuster, 1986).

8. "Alex Haley Biography," *The Kunta Kinte—Alex Haly Foundation*, http://www.kintehaley.org/haleybio.html.

9. Alex Haley, Citation unknown.

10. Reverend Jesse Jackson, quoted on *QuotationsBook*, http://quotationsbook.com/quote/19447/.

11. Robert Half, quoted by Donald P. Wilson in *Total Victory: The Complete Management Guide to a Successful Nlpb Representation Election Campaign* (Labor Relations Institute, Inc., 1998), 203.

SECTION 12: TAKE CHARGE OF YOUR FUTURE
Chapter 44: Life Is Life

1. Benjamin Franklin, quoted by Marilyn Doty in *CMSA of Central Florida eNewsletter*, March, 2007, http://www.centralfloridacmsa.org/docs/Mar_2_CMSA.pdf.

2. "Abraham Maslow," *Wikipedia: The Free Encyclopedia*, http://en.wikipedia.org/wiki/Abraham_Maslow.

3. Barbara Tuchman, quoted in "Philosophy and Attitude Quotes," on *Home-Business-Expert.com*, http://www.home-business-expert.com/Philosophy-and-Attitude-Quotes.html.

4. Thomas Jefferson, quoted on *FamousQuotes.com*, http://www.famousquotes.com/show.php?_id=1030088.

5. Unknown author, quoted by Brian Tracy in *Maximum Achievement: Strategies and Skills That Will Unlock Your Hidden Powers to Succeed* (New York: Simon & Schuster, 1995), 200-01.

Chapter 45: Choose Your Response

1. Wally "Famous" Amos, quoted by Dr. Bessie E. Swann in "Change," *The Mouthpiece eNewsletter*, http://www.wheelerce.org/news/article0.htm.

2. Gloria Estefan, "Seal our Fate," *Into the Light*, Emilio Estefan Jr., Epic Records, http://www.mtv.com/lyrics/estefan_gloria/seal_our_fate/399270/lyrics.jhtml.

3. James Hillman, Citation unknown.

4. Zig Ziglar, Citation unknown.

Chapter 46: Create a Choice Credo

1. Og Mandino, *The Choice* (New York: Bantam, 1986).

2. C.S. Lewis, quoted on *WorldofQuotes.com*, http://www.worldofquotes.com/author/C.-S.-Lewis/1/index.html.

3. Arnold J. Toynbee, quoted on *BrainyQuote.com*, http://www.brainyquote.com/quotes/quotes/a/arnoldjto101735.html.

4. Eleanor Roosevelt, quoted on *thinkexist.com*, http://thinkexist.com/quotation/in_the_long_run-we_shape_our_lives-and_we_shape/13255.html.

Chapter 47: Insist on Internal Accountability

1. Oprah Winfrey, quoted on *The Quotations Page*, http://www.quotationspage.com/quote/1969.html.

2. Mark Twain, quoted on *BrainyQuote*, http://www.brainyquote.com/quotes/quotes/m/marktwain105031.html.

3. Will Rogers, quoted on *The Quotations Page*, http://www.quotationspage.com/quote/2672.html.

ABOUT THE AUTHOR

G LENN VAN EKEREN IS THE Executive Vice President for Vetter Health Services in Omaha, Nebraska, a company committed to providing "dignity in life" for the elderly. For the past thirty years, Glenn's primary profession has been helping people grow. His passion as a leader is to create a work environment where people feel good about themselves, their jobs, the people they work with, the people they serve, and their organization.

As a professional speaker, he is known for his inspiring, enthusiastic, and down-to-earth approach for maximizing people and organizational potential. Glenn has also traveled the country providing more than one thousand seminars and keynotes to nearly one hundred thousand people. Glenn's motto in life is "to live every moment of every day to the fullest." His seminars and books will make you will laugh, think, feel great, look at life in a fresh way, and be inspired to stretch toward your potential. His messages capture people's attention, stir emotions, and provide practical strategies for personal and organizational growth.

Since 1988, Glenn has authored several books, including the original *Speaker's Sourcebook* and the best-selling *Speaker's Sourcebook II, 12 Simple Secrets of Happiness: Finding Joy in Everyday Relationships, 12 Simple Secrets of Happiness at Work: Finding*

Fulfillment, Reaping Rewards, and *12 Simple Secrets of Happiness in a Topsy-Turvy World.* He is a featured author in several *Chicken Soup for the Soul* books, as well as the editor of *Braude's Treasury of Wit & Humor for All Occasions* and *The Complete Speaker's & Toastmaster's Library.* Glenn has penned numerous articles for various professional publications.